MW00899566

MERLE

Unearthed and Rebirthed

John M. Hornsby

John 1:32

B. lair,
Ya gotta die to live.

J
2019

For Kim, who loves me like no other

INTRODUCTION

Summer, 2017

"**G**ood morning...John Hornsby...7 o'clock appointment" I said quietly to the receptionist, intending to keep *my* private procedure – private, you know, special, because in John's world, it's about John. Why should this be any different?

As she examined my information, confirming I was who I said I was, that indeed I had an appointment and was in the correct location, I looked everywhere but at her papers, to show her my knowledge and respect of HIPPA compliance. She wasn't impressed.

Gazing behind me, panning the waiting room side-to-side, *Geez*, I thought. *Surely I'm in the wrong place. What's up with these poor folks? A haggard, hungry-looking bunch; are they not? - Cresting the backside of mid-life, "Over the hill" would be a compliment - Look at that one over there! – Good God...*

"Yes, Mr. Hornsby, we have you down." *What?* Throat punched back into reality, I reassessed the sad sacks behind me. *Who am I kidding? - Aint so special after all. This little black sheep had just found the rest of the herd,* as a good friend of mine would say – *Sigh – Reality sucks.*

We were all *"Over the hill"* and *Dr. Ben Dover,* as he'd humorously nicknamed himself, was about to go over our rivers and through our woods, but his sleigh ride don't lead to grandmother's house, if you know what I mean. He was headed to our dark side, where the sun don't shine; it was colonoscopy time.

"Thanks" as I sheepishly took the redundant paperwork-laden clipboard and found a seat, a good ways from the Men's Room, as I was fairly certain that my "prep" was done prepping. Theologian Billy Ray Cyrus once sang "All gave some, some gave all" and I had given *my* all the night before.

For the record, colonoscopies get a bad rap, *butt* (spelling intentional, for effect) they aren't bad at all. The prep is actually pretty funny (*I'll never outgrow that*) and the drugs are amazing. Years ago, as I readied for my maiden voyage with "Dr. Dover", I asked my Dad what to expect from the prep, as he had undergone many a scope. He grinned and asked if I'd ever seen the space shuttle launch...

Once the junk's out of the trunk and the IV's in, the rest is blessed. You're painlessly out cold for a half-hour or so, and the euphoric, residual effects stick around for a few hours afterward. Not a bad gig. Plus, as a recovering alcoholic, Kim hasn't had to pour me into the passenger seat and drive me home for nearly 27 years. But every three years now she gets to relive those sweet memories of our yesteryear and drive my under-the-influenced-butt home. I still beg her, with slurred speech, to hit Jack-in-the-Box for ninety nine cent tacos, just for old times' sake.

Half-way through the paperwork, Kim by my side, an elderly couple demanded our attention - and everyone else's. The woman was dressed in waiting room-appropriate attire; gray, bell-bottom sweats, fluffy, warm socks, not intended to be worn with shoes but were, and contrasting colored sweatshirt from her granddaughter's university (so proud). With her smartphone at max volume, she was enjoying a video of their grandchildren, over and over and over again, holding it in front of her disinterested husband, passive-aggressively begging him to watch with her, to no avail.

Her husband was engrossed in his own smartphone as if with a much more pressing matter. Legal document? *Nah.* Business deal? *Don't think so.* Defiantly ignoring her pleas, he remained fixated on his phone and tenacious to his task at-hand...selecting a new ring tone.

He sampled them, one-by-one, hundreds it seemed - also at max volume. Actually, there weren't hundreds of options but 53 - we counted them. He tried each of them a number of times, causing me to just about "prep" my seat! Over and over he tried them - then I heard it - Old Phone.

Although he ultimately selected Old Car Horn, go figure, hearing Old Phone instantly took me back, back some*where* and to some*one* I hadn't heard from in a long, long time.

Old phones, originally rotary-dial and available in colors like Harvest Gold, Avocado Green, Beige, Brown and Red, when Commissioner Gordon rang the Bat Cave, were later enhanced by the push-button feature, greatly increasing your odds of being the tenth caller to the radio station and scoring the free concert tickets.

Way short of the color palette, there were two volume options "Loud" and "Louder" or "Can't Afford Hearing Aids" and "Lazarus Come Forth" but they had only one, infamous, never-to-be-forgotten ring tone. Wait for it - You know what's coming... "Clangangangangity...echo, echo...echo... Clangangangangity...echo...echo...echo..."

Before "Clang" met "angangangity" that old man's Old Phone took me to the kitchen of the house I grew up in, where PA9-1594, that white, wall-mounter hung. The receiver smelled like a bouquet of coffee, Certs and ear wax and had one of those extra-long curlicue cords. You remember them - always bunched up and twisted around themselves, hindering your reach just enough to miss the couch and Dad's recliner. And, even when straightened out, they were notorious for breeding those rogue curlicues that went opposite of the rest. They remain a mystery to me.

PA9-1594 was masking-taped and magic-markered on my Charlie Brown lunch box. *So…that's where Mrs. Leggett, my kindergarten teacher, got our number.* She felt the need to ring PA9-1594 one morning to tell Mom why I'd be coming home with a note pinned to my shirt. My Kindergarten class photo has me holding a toy truck, smiling ear to ear with an envelope, dang near the size of my head, pinned to my shirt. It wasn't a "Thank You" note for the Christmas gift Mom had given her, nor a letter of recommendation for my stellar performance in the classroom, although my good buddy, Gready, and I considered my performance rather "stellar" that day. Mom answered the ringer that morning and, in-turn, ran my backside through the ringer that afternoon before Charlie Brown even hit the kitchen counter.

Years later PA9-1594 would ring loud, but not so proud, one afternoon after school. I answered it; shouldn't have. Mr. Deegan, Economics teacher my senior year, asked "…to speak to your Mother". Should've hung up on him when I had the chance. As I heard Mom pick-up in the back bedroom, I pretended to hang up, but didn't, and listened in, when you could still do that. Deegan went on to inform Mom I'd never amount to anything, and I quote "John will obviously never attend Texas A&M and major in Engineering…"

Mom heard about all she needed to hear before letting Deegan have it. She ripped him a new blessed assurance and hung up on him. Having my back and believing in me was something Mom provided for us, always, without exception.

Turned out Deegan was half-right; I *would not* attend Texas A&M and I *did not* major in Engineering, but I *did* amount to something, something wonderful and something Mom is still helping me discover, even to this day.

Also turned out Deegan and I had something in common; he *also* lived at home with his mother - but wasn't seventeen, like me. He was mid-fifties and wasn't "caring for the elderly"; he just breastfed a little longer than most. His mother would bring his little sack lunch that she'd made for him to the school when he'd left it at home. We saw it about twice a week. And *I* wasn't going to amount to anything?

PA9-1594 rang all hours of the day and for all kinds of reasons but if someone dared call the house past 10:00 PM Mom would wonder out loud "Now, who could that be calling after 10 o'clock? It better be an emergency. You don't call people after 10 o'clock unless something's wrong" and that unwritten policy stayed with me.

The older I get the louder my ears ring. Even through my cockleburr, bristle-haired passageways my ears have a constant buzz, hum and ring to them; have for years. When Old Phone sounded off in that Waiting Room that day I finally knew where that ringing was coming from – and who was making the call.

As if ringing from a kitchen far, far away, after 30 long years of silence "Clangangangangity...echo, echo...echo... Clangangangangity...echo...echo...echo..."

From the depths of my lonesome, grieving soul, PA9-1594 was ringing. So, filled with expectant hope, I softly reached for its receiver, palming it gently with my two hands, pressing to my ear and whispered "Hello?"

John, it's me.

THE CALL

8.3.1987

E ight to ten Budweisers, can't recall, into a typical, after-workday evening, a good meal with Kim, dog fed, dishes done and doors locked, we headed down the hallway for a shower and the cool, cotton sheets for some shut-eye.

"Clangangangangity...echo, echo...echo... clangangangangity... echo...echo...echo..."

Without batting an eye, I blurted "Now, who's that calling this time of night? It's damn near 10 o'clock."

Answering our wall-mounted harvest gold I yelled "Hello!" in my *Whoever this is had better have an emergency* voice.

"John - *brief pause* - This is Dad - *cracked voice, quick recovery, cleared throat now matter of fact* - Your Mother's had a stroke." Unknowingly pacing down the hallway, until the tangled cord yanked me backwards, I listened intently as Dad shared the news.

Unable to hear the details, yet knowing something was terribly wrong, Kim embraced me from behind, burying her head between my shoulder blades. Leaning forward I melted into the wall of our hallway as I slumped under the weight of the devastating news.

"We're at Parkland in downtown Dallas" he continued. "She's in good hands - *longer pause* - I've called your brother and sister. Be careful on the road." Kim took the phone from me and hung it up, returning to hug me. Kim held me in that moment the way she, and only one other could - and that *other* lay in a coma at Dallas' Parkland Hospital.

Arriving at Paul's, our brother, he awaited us in his driveway, keys in-hand, pacing impatiently back and forth, closely resembling the blue-suited gentleman awaiting our arrival at Parkland.

Not one of us was stable enough to drive but we had to. Paul took the wheel, I rode shotgun and Kim kept us as calm as possible from the back seat. The drive was a blur, from the car speed and the emotions, but we made it, somehow and in record time. Stuck overnight in Iowa, Cristy, our sister, would catch the first flight south the next morning.

Here's how it went down. Combustion Engineering (CE) was a thriving corporation Dad served for 33 years, rising from entry level ranks to Executive Vice President. When promoted, Mom and Dad left Houston, after 26 years, and relocated to Dallas. They'd only been in Big D a few years before this dreadful night.

Mom was ever the consummate wife, mother and homemaker. She had an undergrad, a four-year degree, in home economics; I'm talking an incarnated June Cleaver for Christ's sake! No one, I mean no one, answered their call nor took their work to heart more seriously than Mom. Dad and we three kids were spoiled rotten by her and wouldn't trade it for the world.

Dad's career was a big deal for him, for Mom and for our family as a whole and significantly influenced our family's lifestyle. We were the Americana family to a tee. Dad was an executive success and Mom the ultimate homemaker with the ultimate home. Country clubs, church membership, civic organizations, Masonic Lodge, Little League Board, PTA, Women's Auxiliary, Team Mom, Den Mother, you get the picture.

John M. Hornsby

Mom and Dad, both, came from humble beginnings; Dad, son of working-class surveyor, realtor (more of a horse trader) and rancher and Mom was a Baptist preacher's kid, a P.K. as they're called. Neither of them had two nickels between them when they married, but loved each other completely and built a life together, a family and a home that we kids were privileged to be raised in.

Cristy and I are both nostalgic hoarders. We hang on to stuff that's meaningful to us; doesn't matter if it's meaningful to anyone else. It's a personal thing.

She recently shared with us a storage box, telling me "Just take it and read through it...You'll thank me later" Reluctantly I took it from her, as I'm trying to knock it down a notch, but once I looked inside I couldn't thank her enough.

The plastic tote box was loaded with hundreds of old letters that I never knew existed. Glad she had them and not Dad; he would've tossed them away years ago; not big on nostalgia. As if reading a romance novel from the '40's, the letters were between Mom and Dad. They wrote to each other every single weekday between January 1947 and May 1948, only skipping the weekends, Christmas breaks and summers as they were both in college at the time.

The Pony Express was on a hot streak between Austin and Belton for a year and a half. The words they wrote to each other showed me how it all began. It now makes sense. Few couples have experienced such unconditional love, commitment and self-sacrifice as Mom and Dad enjoyed with each other. We kids were lucky.

Dad travelled quite a bit, entertained a lot and was always, always busy with his work, which was the RPM he ran at best, but always seemed to be there when it mattered. *Still don't know how he did that so well.*

Mom not only appreciated Dad's provision for our family but

supported and celebrated it in extraordinary ways. I mean, there's a picture in our family photo album of Dad proudly holding an apple pie Mom had scratched out one afternoon in the kitchen, celebrating a big contract Dad had negotiated. The pie had the company logo of Dad's customer carved into the crust! She didn't order it or stop by Costco on the way home; she handmade the thing, just to let him know how proud she was of him and his work. Who does that?

While living in Dallas, as Dad neared his 30th year anniversary with CE, Mom planned a huge surprise party for him to celebrate that milestone, inviting his corporate leadership and co-workers. Flying in from across the country, the suits and their spouses arrived in Dallas the afternoon of August 3rd. Being a company celebration, we kids weren't on the guest list, but those who worked for Dad and those whom Dad worked for were all there, about thirty in all.

As Dad would tell the story, he had returned to Dallas from a contract negotiation he'd been finalizing up north. Mom picked him up at a private hangar adjacent to Love Field in Dallas. Dressed to the nines she told him she'd like to take him to dinner to celebrate his 30th year with the company.

"Hon', that's so sweet of you, but let's just go home and relax together. No need for anything fancy like that". She persisted. He caved. They arrived at Lawry's, a fine-dining, Dallas steakhouse, valet parked and requested a table for two. Unbeknownst to him, Mom already had a large dining room reserved and filled with his surprise guests.

As the hostess guided them to their table the double doors to the dining room opened wide and Ed and Clo were greeted by a thunderous "Surprise!" As always, Mom pulled it off magnificently. Dad was overwhelmed by the surprise, the size of the party and the ever-supportive love from his sweet Clo.

When retelling the story, not often at all, emotionally he'd say

"We looked at each other, in that moment..." His grief would overtake him – then he'd continue as he wept "She loved me so...and was so proud of me..." and that would be it.

Ed and Clo saved the best for last. Their eyes first met December 19, 1946 then, one last time, August 3, 1987. Mom collapsed right then and there, in front of them all – as *our* world collapsed right along with her. That would be the worst "Surprise!" we've ever had.

In the chaos that erupted, Dad instinctively gathered her into his arms, rushing her outside to their car, which hadn't yet been valeted. Dad's right-hand man, Al, and his wife, drove Mom and Dad to Parkland Hospital, Ed holding his "Sweet Clo", his "Best gal", tightly in his arms in the backseat. Once in the hands of the Emergency Room doctors, E.S. Hornsby was escorted to the appropriately-titled Waiting Room, his supporters gathering, full-force, in his wake and by his side, awaiting our arrival.

2:45 A.M. - Parkland Hospital. "ICU?" I yelled, as we stormed the Emergency Room. "Thanks..." We three raced down that long, seemingly endless, sterile, hallway, that same hallway in every hospital, and most nightmares, that runs as fast as you do, even faster sometimes, its end unreachable.

Turning the corner we stopped dead in our tracks at the entrance of the ICU Waiting Room...There he was, seated, protectively surrounded by his ever-present entourage, The Suits, I call them; blues, grays, pinstriped, white shirted and Windsor-knotted. Brando and Pacino would have fit right in. Silent - Somber - All-business – The room smelled of coffee, sterile hand wash and Vitalis.

The Suits surrounded Dad like the faithful followers they were; his boss seated at his right hand, a follower of Dad's as well. Their stoic expression hailed their allegiance to Dad but even more so their love for Mom. They knew the rock on which E.S. Hornsby stood. They were there when the rock crumbled...and as he did, as well.

Humbly in the corner, within reach yet appropriately apart from the others, arms crossed with his forearm upright, hand supporting his chin as in deep thought, present, silently present, in a suit of a different shade of gray, with crimson tie and white shirt stood Dr. Charles Cook, Mom and Dad's Pastor.

We hadn't really known Brother Cook, as we were taught to address our pastors, nor experienced an exhibition of grace, compassion and authentic pastoring, until that moment. I wouldn't realize, until many years later, how much I learned from Brother Cook that night and the days that followed.

Another quiet soul, somberly standing in the opposite corner of the waiting room, right where he wanted, out of the way, in the shadows of the others who needed more of the limelight, was Dad's best friend, a little brother of sorts, Bob; hands sheepishly withdrawn deep into the front pockets of his well-worn Levis. Bob was the smartest guy in the room, by a country mile, but needed no one to know that. He probably didn't believe it himself.

Both of Dad's pastors, Brother Cook and Bob, were positioned just where he needed them - and would he ever need them...

Upon our arrival Dad's disciples extended their care and concern before excusing themselves; their job was done and done well. Dad was a lone ranger but didn't do well alone, if that makes sense. Now with his family, Dad was safe again. The two pastors never left our side.

As the docs would inform us, Mom had suffered a massive cerebral hemorrhage. Likely born with it, it went 60 years undetected, then, like an uninvited guest, it showed up and crashed the party, hers and ours. Parkland's finest had done their good work; Mom was "stabilized and resting comfortably".

Dad led me, Kim and Paul into her room. As we turned the corner, past the drawn curtain surrounding her bed, I saw her

- and couldn't take it in. I was unable and incapable of understanding what I was seeing. How could the woman I was just talking to the day before be laying there, right in front of us yet a million miles from us? It made no sense.

We'd had Dad's surprise birthday party for his 60th just a few months before. She had driven herself to San Antonio just two months ago to have dinner with Kim and me for our first wedding anniversary. They gave us a new lawn mower. What is happening? I wondered to myself.

The room had all the bells and whistles of someone not doing well, typical ICU; loud beeps, monitors, alarms, machines, people coming and going, no one talking much, just in and out doing their good work. *This is all wrong – All messed up,* as I stared at her.

Her body lay completely still...Only her chest moved... expanding up, up, up...and collapsing back down...up, up, up... back down as the ventilator manipulated her lungs. As I stood at her side, Kim hugging my right arm, head resting on my shoulder, I couldn't take my eyes off of hers. Her beautiful, hazel eyes, that once *saw* you, that smiled within themselves and could brighten your darkest day, assuring you everything would be ok, were now dark, glassy and staring into nowhere... and offered no assurance whatsoever that we'd be ok.

I could see she truly *was* "resting comfortably" but not there – elsewhere. She was gone. She had left and wasn't coming back - and we knew it - and words have yet to be created that describe the emptiness, hopelessness and grief that introduced themselves in that moment.

I knew the Bible, went regular to church, been there and bought the t-shirt, but none of that was offering any sense of solace whatsoever right about then. Knowing your loved one is "With God now" is comforting, kind of, but did nothing for the pain I felt in the here and now. There was nothing *sweet* about her sweet bye and bye. It hurt like Hell.

Above the noise of the ICU, an Arkansas-sweet tea of a voice whispered...

> *Ye shall seek me, and shall not find me: and where I am, thither ye cannot come...In my Father's house are many mansions...I go to prepare a place for you...that where I am, there ye may be also... and lo, I am with you alway, even to the end of the age.*

She knew the red letters well...

Cristy would later tell us, although not with us at the time, she knew before she boarded the Dallas-bound airplane Mom was gone. She just knew.

Settling back into the waiting room we sat silently, except for the occasional "Can I get anyone anything?" as one of us would go for coffee. ICU waiting rooms have their own vibe, and they're all about the same. Everyone's down, worried, anxious, pessimistically hopeful, exhausted, cotton-mouthed, malnourished but not hungry, caffeine-high, bad-breathed – you've been there.

As we sat there, in the twilight hours of August 4th Dad, dazing at the floor tile, three in front and two to the right of him, broke the silence with "This is the first thing in my life that I couldn't control". What a telling statement he made - and one that I'd recall many, many times in the years to come.

Just outside the doorway of the Waiting Room stood Brother Cook, far enough away to give us space yet close enough to listen. He'd heard Dad's comment. Looking over at him, he said nothing but made a mental note of it, no doubt. *Always wondered if he ever circled back to Dad on that one. I hope so.*

I spent some quality time with Brother Cook in that hallway. That's where I learned that "Everything does NOT happen for a reason". Swimming in my confusion, thrown overboard without a life jacket, I needed some answers, some closure, and there were none to be found. I sauntered up to Brother Cook and with a heavy dose of false-confidence said "Well, everything happens for a reason" to which he replied "No, John, it doesn't. There are many, many things in life that just *are*. Life happens and no one is exempt from it. God can do amazing work in us as we experience the ups and downs of life, but everything doesn't happen *for* a reason".

He would have no idea how his reply would impact me then, and for the ministry I would eventually be called to. I could have retired ten years ago if I had a buck for every time I've told a hurting soul that same thing in an ICU waiting room.

Cristy did arrive the following day, around Noon. We picked her up at DFW Airport and rushed to get back to Parkland, telling ourselves "We have to get there in time", knowing full well she was already gone.

Upon arrival, we took Cristy back to be with Mom. Nothing had changed. She looked the same. No progress, no digress. Up, up, up...Down...Up, up, up...Down...

The head doc came to speak to the family, calling us into that special consult room nobody wants to go in. Dad was first out of the chute, intending to sound strong and in control, but came off just as he was, brokenhearted and helpless.

"She and I talked about this many, many times and she does not want to live like this..." - *Choked up, followed by futile attempts to get himself under control* - "So, if we need to cease any more live-saving measures..." *Shaking and sobbing uncontrollably...*

The doc's empathic hand reached for Dad's shoulder - "Mr. Hornsby, thank you for that, but in cases like your wife's, there's no decision to make. Without the ventilator breathing for her, she will not be able to live any longer...Honestly speaking, sir, your wife went peacefully and painlessly in the restaurant, very likely without knowing or feeling any of it".

There were no words that Dad needed any more, in that moment, than those. We are forever grateful for that graceful doc and his Good Work that day, August 4, 1987.

One last time, one last kiss on her forehead, one last everything - we held her hands as the machines went silent. The nurse closed her eyelids for us and she became stiller than any still I'd ever seen. Peaceful – Serene - At rest....And the rest of us, thrown into a freefall with no bottom in sight.

What did I *really* lose? I knew *who* I had lost, but *what* did I lose? These unanswered, unasked questions plagued my soul, for the next 31 years.

Don't go looking for the reasons

Don't go asking Jesus Why?

We're not meant to know the answers

They belong to the by and by

Chris Stapleton

THE SERVICES

Returning home, word got out. Relatives and close friends were notified and began the post-mortem process of awkward know-not-what-to-say, "If there's anything we can do…", "Had she been ill…?", "God now has another angel" visits. Much-appreciated and well-intended we were glad they all came by. Dad needed some distraction.

Mom was everywhere in the house; she had just left the afternoon before to meet Dad at the airport; now she was the reason we gathered. Her yard shoes still by the back door, lipstick and folded Kleenex on the kitchen counter as she had cleaned her purse before leaving. We expected to see her in the kitchen, playing hostess, as she did so well. We sucked at it. Mom would have had a buffet and serving area for the food. We had an ice chest buffet with cold beer. I helped myself to our buffet for it fed me the only peace I could find.

Unsure who planned the funerals but someone did. We had a gathering at Mom and Dad's Methodist Church; Brother Cook did the service. Then we migrated south to Austin for another service there, as Mom and Dad considered Austin "Home". Most of it was an emotional blur.

Leaving San Antonio in a frenzy the night of Dad's call, I hadn't taken a suit, or Kim a dress. Mom's funeral was not on our minds at the time. Kim was so sweet and found a beautiful dress in

Mom's closet. She, in that dress, was exactly what I needed at the time. I wore one of Dad's suits, with the waist tied in a knot in the back and the cuffs a good 3 inches above a pair of his best Johnston Murphy tasseled loafers. Mine hadn't made the trip.

Brother Cook was wonderful, at both services, providing a calming presence amidst our anxious environment. Family and friends came from all around to pay their respects to Clo Hornsby and comfort us in ways we couldn't have imagined. We remain truly grateful.

Never big on open-caskets, Dad made sure his Clo would have her privacy during the services, but we wanted to see her one last time. In a private viewing, Paul, Cristy, Kim and I saw her. But an empty shell, her body lay there in front of us as she rested elsewhere. On the very bosom from which we fed I laid my prized possession, my trophy rodeo buckle. Not sure why; I just needed to pay tribute to her somehow, some way. Polished shiny as the day I was awarded it, I laid it to her chest as if laying my treasure at her feet.

Another long-time Austin friend of Mom and Dad's, Uncle Don we called him, toured the cemetery for us and selected Mom's burial plot. He picked a double plot, at Dad's request, for them to be joined together again one day, side-by-side, as they both wanted.

With both the Dallas and Austin services now complete, we gathered around that double plot on that hot August afternoon for Mom's burial. Our grandparents, Dad's folks, are buried just a short walk from where we stood, along with our aunt and one of our cousins. Theirs' too were untimely deaths; too young and out-of-sequence. I'd been to all of those funerals; some I remembered attending, some I was too young and didn't. Here we were, yet again, too early in life, burying our dear Mother.

It was a typical scene, green outdoor carpet and little white chairs, a canopy to shade a dozen or so, gathered guests dressed in black, her casket displayed as if on an altar, flowers and sprays galore, a mound of freshly dug dirt and a six-foot hole that would bury her much further from us and plunge us into an abyss we knew nothing about.

"Amen" and "Thank you for coming...This concludes our service" dismissed us as we hugged friends and distant relatives and "promised to stay in touch" before going our separate ways.

As I looked down into that hole, up and down its four sides, layered sod, top soil, clay and caliche, and the box that would be lowered into it, I felt I was being interned into a hole of my own, resting in a box of my own that had been built long before then.

There's no right time, nor right way, for a loved one to pass, and Mom's unexpected death sucker-punched Dad bad. He and Mom had been planning their well-deserved, early retirement, designing their place in the country. Back in Dallas he laid out the design drawings on their living room coffee table and presented us with their dream, where they'd planned to live out their golden years together.

Slamming his pencil on the blueprints, in sorrowful anger, he turned his back on the table and walked away, in response to his hopeless uncertainty. The absolute, unquestionable love of his life was in the grave...and their future right along with her. E.S. Hornsby was a lost soul.

Clark Kent went back in the phone booth and suited up. In Dad's way, he immediately reverted back to Superman, his persona of choice, and the man of steel was back at it, busier than ever. Superman tights on Dad covered up a lot more than love handles and dun-lap; they concealed his grief and contained his pain, not to be touched, never to be discussed. Even he dared not go near it.

Suited back up, Dad downshifted and hammered the gas. Ditching retirement and their place in the country, he accepted another promotion with CE, engaged in another relationship, ultimately marrying, and moved to the northeast. For him, a rolling stone gathers no grief. For us, the rolling stone was ungatherable.

With Mom gone, and Dad almost as gone, I withdrew as well for the better part, or worst, of the next five years, slipping further into *my* persona of choice, a red, white and blue 12-ounce superhero suit of my own. My alcohol consumption hit an all-time high, and low, though never high-enough to reach her nor low low-enough to shake the sorrow.

I could only stay in the air so long, so like a pilot who'd lost an engine, losing fuel and losing control, spiraling downward in a drunken descent, I prepared for a crash landing, searching far and wide for the safest place to set *me* down. Calling the ball on a runaway carrier navigating its own stormy sea in the dead of night, with a glimmer of a landing light in view, I hit the deck of the U.S.S. Ed Hornsby dead-center.

Though my emotional wreckage demanded repairs his carrier wasn't equipped to make, that didn't stop me from coming in and didn't stop him from letting me. I desperately wanted back what I had lost, the unconditional love of my mother, and he was the only parent I had left, so it seemed logical to land there – But grief often trumps logic.

After a few years of awkward, failed attempts to emotionally draw Dad close to me I stopped trying and resorted to the only thing I knew, and knew all too well, that would keep us near one another, complete compliance. Back in The Box, the box the therapists call The Good Son Syndrome.

Dad would tell us that he raised us with a "tight grip on a long leash". His grip needed not be tight with me because I stayed in close range of him, leaving plenty of slack in the leash. Walking by his side had gotten me plenty of "Atta boys" and pats on the head in the past. Surely this would work again now, when I needed it the most.

Being a "Good Son" and it being its own "Syndrome" in no way implies that my sister and brother are prodigals; they just had more courage to be *themselves*. Me? Not so much. I chose the easier, softer path.

As a chip off the old block, I'd like the things he liked and not like the things he didn't like. I'd dress like him and work like him and act like him and drink like him. This wouldn't be difficult at all – I'd been doing it all my life. And, honestly, it would be easier for both us. So, back in The Box I went.

> *I'm the man in the Box*
>
> *Buried in my shit*
>
> *Won't you come and save me?*
>
> *Save me*
>
> *Alice in Chains*

THE BOX DAD BUILT

Hello walls…Hello window…Hello ceiling…

We must all stick together or else I'll lose my mind

I've got a feeling she'll be gone a long, long time

Faron Young

Truly worth a thousand words, pictures, photographs, portraits, whatever you want to call them, say a lot. They say what the photographers want them to say, and what the photographees want you to hear. But, oh if they could really speak…

While in Houston, for the memorial service for Gready's mother, one of a few second Moms to me, I arrived early at the mausoleum and toured a bit, as I'm apt to do. Cemeteries and the like fascinate me and this one did more than most others. Walking the long, granite and marble-lined halls of this mausoleum, through the aroma of star-gazers, birds of paradise, plastic wreaths and death funk I came upon quite the shrine; a couple's double-monument burial vault, inset and velvet-rope barricaded, a gated community of sorts - for the dead.

Adorning each side of this display were two portraits, or oil paintings I couldn't tell, of the couple, not together but separate; husband on the far left, his wife to the right and neither of

John M. Hornsby

them had died in the 1960's when these pics were shot. Per their monument he'd knocked off a young 73, she, north of 85, but per their portraits, they were in their prime.

Hair parted perfectly, slicked back, tail-whipped in front, her-ringbone jacket, black trousers, left hand in the front pocket, right hand holding a candela wrapped Antonio y Cleopatra cigar. I recognized it right off. Dad chewed and smoked those for years, stashing them in the slide cabinet behind his recliner. Clandestinely hidden, logoed on the underside of the box lid, Cleopatra laid naked. The National Geographics were two shelves up. A boy has to start somewhere.

He was sheer confidence...No...arrogance, letting me, and everyone else who passed by, know that he was in complete control... of everything. Successful? Oh, he was successful. Utter satisfaction...One to be admired...but he was dead.

His wife, never to be known otherwise, looked much the same. Ball gown, white gloved...Sophisticated...Made-up...Complete, but only with him...Her eyes, softly and admiringly, looked dir-ectly across their monument... at him. He looked upward a bit, above it all...a visionary was he...a vision-heiress was she.

Once beautiful but now dried roses, potpourri material, drooped lifelessly over their vase's rim. - They hadn't been visited in years.

The couple's photographs weren't uncommon for most fam-ilies throughout the post-war era, namely the late 40s through the 70s. Most men looked like him and most women like her. The Americana family had it all together, with pictures to prove it. The patriarch "Father" seated in "his" chair, in the formal living room (not the den), with faithful wife, hair salon-coifed, immaculately-nailed hand resting affectionately and re-spectfully on his shoulder, their well-groomed, appropriately-dressed children standing subordinately behind him, all smil-ing confidently and contently with deep gratitude for "Father's" provision and community prominence.

These family portraits, enlarged life-size, hung either over their brick fireplace mantle or floral-patterned sofa in their formal living room (again, not the den). The 8 x 10 that came in the package was framed and prominently displayed on the credenza (outdated by ten years or more) in "Father's" office, where he held a "good job". The Hornsbys were captain of the team.

Furthering this image of prosperity, the family portraits were taken by a professional, Olin Mills or the like. We were posed and positioned, as play-actors on a movie set, as the director would create the image...of familial integrity, wholesomeness, stability and promise. Olin Mills touched up a lot more than the red dots in our eyes. Framed, matted and bordered, the family portrait portrayed alright – it portrayed The Box.

From the research I've done, post-war America needed the Americana family, and its image was by design. It was paramount for returning servicemen and servicewomen to feel safe and secure in their homes, therefore the family unit and its subsequent structure was at the forefront, each family member having their defined role. Plus, from what I understand, the United States wanted to send a message to its enemies, foreign and domestic, that we had it together and were not to be messed with – ever again.

At the risk of overstating this, but to make a general point, for the most part, women managed the household and, if mothers, they raised the children (kids were from goats back then; wholesome families had "children") while supporting their husband and *his* career, all the while maintaining their outward appearance, as a compliment to *his* appearance. "Trophy wife" is not a modern concept.

Husbands capitalized on their GI Bills and pursued higher education from "reputable" universities that led to highly compensated, long-tenured careers, while knowing their wife had everything under control at home. He could drink, smoke, cuss, have a gut, whatever, as long as he dressed well, drove a nice car and brought home the bacon. "Trophy husband" looks much different.

The kids were "kept in line", behaviorally, academically, athletically and socially, learning the ways of their parents and fruitfully multiplying more of the same, in the appropriate sequence of military service, higher education and a properly planned wedding ceremony at the St. Whomever Church and reception at the Oak Whatever Country Club.

Americana family had stable jobs, nice houses, manicured lawns, cars that were washed and serviced, barbers and beauticians you knew by name, a maid and membership to exclusive clubs, church being one of them. Part of the image was where you "transferred your membership to and from".

Smudge the image and there's a price to pay. Long hair, unshaven face, un-shined shoes, un-edged sidewalks, un-mowed lawn, un-weeded flower beds, double-digit dress size, crooked teeth, acne. Let's take a look...Hmmmm...Ahhhhh...Nope. Not in the portrait. "Get your act together! There, now...say 'cheese'"...

The Buddhists wisely say that a good portion of our suffering stems from attachments and aversions. When attached to something good we fight tooth and nail to remain attached to that something good. Similarly, we fight just as tooth and nail to avert negative things that threaten us. No wonder we pay so much attention to our teeth and nails.

Ed and Clo worked hard to breakaway and build a life together, and they did, well. Be that as it may, and although great people and parents, they posed us for the family portrait just the same, and we reaped all that was sown from it, teeth, nails and all, mainly from Dad.

TEN YEARS AFTER

A Space in Time

Your soul is aching, you can't see it through

But time is healing each day you do

Keep looking forward, forget the past

It's up to you now, don't let it last

Ten Years After

C risty and Paul grew up like twins then I came along, ten years after. Paul drove a super cool blue, custom van with surf racks on top. There was an 8-track tape he played over and over in that van on the way to Quintana Beach and Surfside. Why I remembered this band and this title, I can't tell you, but it was Ten Years After – A Space in Time. Remember it like it was yesterday. Maybe I could relate, being the kid brother to them both.

Watching them color outside the lines of the family portrait, I took copious notes along way, well before I knew what "copious" meant. What resulted was my list - my list of what-to-dos and what-not-to-dos. Cristy and Paul appeared much more willing to take Dad's heat. I wanted no part of it. My list would become my safe place, The Box within which I found security and rested comfortably throughout my childhood, teenage years and young adult life. For me, returning to it after Mom's passing was the fastest way home.

Living the life of a Good Son requires regular assessment of the requirements. Things change. Dads change. My list needed updating now and then. As a small kid I exhibited some athletic skills that seemed to impress Dad, so I went with that for a while. Baseball was his favorite...so, go figure, mine too.

I could swing from both sides of the plate early on and play catch with him in the backyard at an early age. Any kid will take one in the palm of the glove if their Dad is playing with them. Little League eligibility came around at eight years of age and I played every year until almost sixteen.

Baseball was seasonal though. Besides playing catch in the yard, how was I to keep him around in the off-season? My peak season as a Good Son is as follows.

Like it was yesterday, I recall the morning I proudly made my profession of faith to Dad that I liked country music. I'd listened to just about everything my sister and brother grew up listening to, The Rolling Stones, The Doors, Cream and the Lettermen, but I had no music of my own...until then.

As he sped through the Study, heading out the door and to the office, I told him of my decision to turn my will and my life over to Charlie Pride and Ronnie Milsap as my lords and saviors. Stopped him dead in his tracks.

Cocking his head slowly to the side, he smiled and nodded approvingly. Then, in slow motion, for effect, he reached out his right hand, stopping short to make me reach for his, and shook my hand firmly, saying "I like both kinds of music; Country and Western". I was in...

Charlie and Ronnie got me to third base with Dad but Walt

Garrison drove me home. When Walt convinced us that "pure tobacco pleasure" comes from "a pinch between your cheek and gum" Dad threw his plug tobacco down and went for the iconic round tin of the wintergreen wonder. *As Dad did, John did.* At the tender age of ten the hind-pocket on my jeans and little league pants bore the badge of honor, the coveted circle worn white from the bulging can of snuff.

At the time, some of me was real, authentic and genuine. My love for manual labor came along in my DNA I guess. Garage work, ranch work, tearing stuff up and building it back again made Johnboy a happy camper; still does. But, being city-bred and city-born, where did my affection for cowboy boots, tooled leather belts, buckles and feed store caps come from? Barbara Mandrel was "Country when country wasn't cool" but I was neither country nor cool, so why do I like those things? Good question…and a lingering one that I've asked myself for years.

I'd professed my musical faith to Dad and was spittin' out the side window just like him but I needed the goods to go with it, the uniform. So for my 13th birthday, I asked to go to Griffith's Western Wear in Austin, Texas for some gear…and gear I got.

I came out of Griffith's with boots, belt, buckle, snap shirt and a chocolate brown grizzly hat that I'd give my left one to have again. I looked like the urban cowboy, city kid I was but I couldn't have cared less. I fit in…with a very small crowd of others around school…and Dad. I wore that *costume* every day to school – but of course a suit and tie on Sundays to church - just like Dad.

As a youngster, although I didn't know much about theology and such, I'd been in Church every Sunday after Wednesday after Sunday after Wednesday enough to know the scriptures pretty good. And, as I hit puberty and started thinking on my own a bit, I began to ask myself a question.

During a Sunday evening service, closed out by the Lord's Super and budget/finance committee report, the sermon was from "Mark's gospel, chapter 8, verse 36 and following...and if you're with me say 'I am'"..."I am".

What shall it profit a man, if he shall gain the whole world, and lose his own soul?

As Brother So and So went on and on with his theologically impressive dissertation about the "meaning" of this passage, even as the youngster I was, I began to wonder, *You can't gain the whole world...and you can't lose your soul...at least that's what he said last Sunday...It's red-lettered so it must be good...Gain the whole world... lose your own soul...*

That passage stayed with me. Catching my attention as a kid (I mean child) I continued to ponder that passage into my adult life.

Oh, there were rare occasions when my truer self would make an appearance, only to realize that the song remained the same and he would withdraw back down into The Box.

Summer, 1979 I was a painter's helper for my brother, who had a good business doing that early in his career. I'd spent the past few summers in Austin with him, working, skateboarding, drinking beer, throwing Frisbees, doings stuff hippies do in Austin. That summer, July 28th to be exact, landed a blow or two to my Good Son Syndrome, but way short of the knockout it needed.

The Allman Brothers Band had launched a comeback tour and they played Manor Downs, outside of Austin, on July 28th, 1979. Paul had scored three tickets; one each for him, his wife and me. Paul was, and is, a concert pro, having seen many legendary musicians throughout his life, including Stevie Ray Vaughan multiple times, and Led Zeppelin to name a couple. Being a country music suck-up at the time, I hadn't heard much about The Allman Brothers, but, like it was with Dad, if Paul did it...I wanted to do it.

Much too young to experience Woodstock, this was the closest I'd ever come to something like it; probably wasn't, but for a 15 year old wannabe it was Woodstockish enough.

Hanging out in Austin back in the day was cool. There were long-haired, pot smoking, sandal-wearing hippies everywhere and I thought they were the greatest thing I'd ever seen. Out at the lake we had Hippie Hollow, but, arriving at Manor Downs, seeing the multitudes of them gathered for the concert, I felt I'd arrived in Hippie Heaven.

It was a blanket-on-the-ground affair and we'd brought all the necessities, ice chest, quilt, food, etc. for such an event, again he was a pro. As a growing 15-year old, I couldn't get enough to eat, so I worried that the food supply might deplete early in the evening. Not to worry, the hippies like to share everything, and the families on either side of us didn't even ask; they just took a few handfuls of their food for themselves and passed it on around. I gladly accepted and did the same. *So, that's how Jesus fed the multitudes with just five loaves and a couple of fish...he was a hippie.*

Manor Downs 1979 is also where I learned where the term "Pot-luck" came from. Food wasn't the only thing the hippies passed around to their neighbors...*Now that I think about it, maybe it wasn't my age that created my appetite...*

The people-watching was at an all-time "high", and I don't use that term loosely. Seemed every dude had a beard, every chick a tank-top and bras were prohibited on the grounds. As the late-afternoon wore on, many of the tank tops were confiscated as well. Free love was in effect on every other blanket or so and the medic tent was setting up for those who'd overindulged. They would do a good amount of business that night.

With the early evening sun still shining Jerry Jeff Walker took the stage and played a few of his Texas Country tunes; I recognized one or two. Those hippies didn't take too kindly to JJW and dang near booed him off the stage. He endured it, finish-

John M. Hornsby

ing his brief set, and wasted no time getting off-stage...then, *he* arrived.

The sun had set, over the hills west of Austin, the stage lights brightened and Johnny Winter took the stage. Manor Downs erupted into the party I'd hoped it would be...and I was too young and dumb to even know what to hope for. What I soon discovered was that Johnny Winter could make music from that funky-shaped guitar that I'd never heard before...and I loved it.

I'd been messing around with the guitar for a couple of years by that time, taking lessons and learning the basics, but I had no real connection to any style or genre. I picked out a few Charlie Pride tunes to impress Dad, and Paul had taught me a Cream bass line or two, but, other than that, I was learning a few popular song intros (Roundabout and Stairway to Heaven) to impress chicks at school.

As usual, I wanted a guitar just off-center from what was popular. Guitar guys I hung out with played either Strats or Les Pauls but I wanted a 335...because it was different and I'd seen it on a few album covers in Pauls' collection.

I got my 1971 Walnut-finished Gibson ES-335 when I was 13. Bought it used at a local shop. Wasn't a big deal back then as it was only about five years old at the time. You have no idea what I'd give to have that guitar back.

As the white-haired blues master finished his set, to the Manor Downs-full thunderous applause, we made a run to the port-o-cans. The lines were long and the hippies exhibited their common courtesy to their brothers and sisters, which we all were to them, by either patiently waiting (weed has its benefits) in line...or just peeing wherever they happened to be at the time. I was digging the laid-back vibe there. Not a lot of rules and not a lot of trouble; just a lot of good folks having a good time with some good music.

Peeing behind the port-o-cans, allowing someone else to have my place in line (considering the interests of others, as Jesus encouraged us) we made our way back to our quilt and readied for the main attraction, The Allman Brothers Band.

As if the clouds had parted and Christ was returning, the crowd went wild as Gregg, Dickie and the band hit the stage. Dickie was shouldering a red Gibson ES-335 and I was hooked, forevermore. I was crushing on Johnny Winter already but Dickie Betts was another soul I'd never seen the likes of and I couldn't get enough. It truly was a life-changing experience.

As awesome older brothers do, Paul took me "down front, closer to the stage". Making our way through the standing, shoulder-to-shoulder crowd of mellowed-out hippies, we landed by one of the stage light platforms; a scaffold-built structure of sorts where the spotlight guys were mounted. There was maybe two or three of them up there, with another guy "riding shotgun" so to speak.

Paul informed me that some badass biker gang had been hired as "crowd control". One of them hung onto the top of the platform ladder, whacking people with a bat who tried to climb higher for a better view of the stage. Zacchaeus wouldn't have made it up the sycamore tree had that biker been up there. We wisely chose to stay down low.

Down front, close enough to see Dickie Betts rip that Gibson was a bucket list experience I checked at an age too young to know what a bucket list was. I'll remember it forever. I picked out parts to Jessica when I got home.

The Allman Brothers Band was promoting their new album Enlightened Rogues. Leaving that concert I was determined to become an "enlightened rogue" myself, but still having no clue how.

As you can imagine, for a while after returning home to Houston, I was growing my hair longer, wear "cords" (corduroy Levis) and listening to more southern rock 'n roll and blues. *My 335 and I would bond and I'd learn to play like Dickie; be my own kind of soul*, do our own thang, I fantasized.

That lasted about as long as the supper table, where I was reminded about The Box; I left the table more of a *disheartened* than *enlightened* rogue. When away from the vine, the branches wither. Manor Downs was too far away from the pull and pressure of The Box back home.

Well, since I'll have to tell Johnny, Dickie and Gregg I won't be touring with them, and the hippies must Frisbee-on without me...Maybe rodeo would do it, I thought to myself. *I mean, I already have the outfit...and I dip Copenhagen...and listen to both kinds of music, country and western...and, I know a couple of guys that are riding bulls on Thursday nights, getting their pictures taken...and chicks seemed to dig it....Dad will dig it too!...* I convinced myself.

After only a few bucks out of the chute I became more comfortable getting on the backs of slow-bucking bulls...and *very* comfortable boasting about it at school on Fridays...and at home to Dad. I wasn't very good at it so when the photographer would come behind the bucking chutes taking orders for pictures, I'd tell him "Ya, I'd like one...but you'd better be quick because I don't stay on very long..." I wasn't joking.

Riding bulls, better yet the pictures of me riding bulls, impressed Dad, so I kept at it, never staying on long enough to really have the chance of getting hurt too bad, but long enough to win the high school rodeo team bull riding series, which awarded me the buckle I mentioned.

Being an undiagnosed/un-medicated ADHD terrible student and teenage alcoholic, I wasn't headed to A&M to study engineering, as Mr. Deegan had already prophesied. I followed a chick into the Sam Houston State University room at our high school's college and career day. Never saw her again, but did learn that SHSU had a rodeo team and *that* got my attention.

Taking the SAT with the worst hangover of my life, I was accepted at SHSU and made my way to Huntsville for college... actually for rodeoing and beer drinking. I was on the honor roll at both.

Never a top performer, I did ok and rode bulls and bareback broncs my five years at SHSU, winning a long round or two along the way. Dad loved it and was proud to tell his friends and business associates about my rodeoing. But, honestly, my *heart* wasn't in it; I was only in it for the parties, friendships and Dad's approval.   If you added up the accumulative time I stayed onboard a bucking bull or bareback bronc, over eight years and hundreds of nods at the chute gate, I *might* have had eight seconds total.

Our college rodeo coach asked once, after double-grabbing on a good bronc at the A&M rodeo "Hornsby, you just can't stand prosperity; can you? You make the prettiest 6-second rides I've ever seen, and then bail out for some reason..." He had no idea how he had summed up my entire life.

At that time in my life, I was a boots and jeans, Birdwell Beach Britches, snap shirt, butt cut-haired, snuff-dipping, surfer, rodeo cowboy wannabe who was trying hard to be his Dad, older brother or some hybrid of the two, with still no clue who the authentic John was.

My freshman year in college, a good summer went bad as I made some poor choices that damn near killed me and a few others. As he always did, Dad rescued me and kept me from facing any of the consequences I so deserved...and deeply needed to experience.

Home for the summer, healing from the accident, and from being treated like a little boy, I did some soul-searching. *I'd rededicate to my faith, my real faith not country music, and get outta that damn Box once and for all...*I decided.

Finding a Christian bookstore, (a pro shop of sorts where Christians stock up on messiah merch and soothe our soul from the night before; at least that's why I was in there) I landed on a cool Ichthys sticker with Jesus' name in the center. Subconsciously shoving my t-shirt sleeve up, I held the Ichthys to my upper right arm and nodded slowly in self-approval that it would be the perfect tribute to my spiritual rededication, in the form of a tattoo.

The Yellow Pages were stored along with the White Pages in the cabinet beneath our wall-mounted push-button. I pulled them, rolled the pages to find...ahhhh..."Tattoo". There were only a few shops listed, not the cast of thousands we see today. There's about as many tattoo shops as there are churches and Chick-fil-A's these days.

My tattoo shop choice was buried in the bowels of Houston off of Montrose Street. The city map got me there in no time and I, and my Ichthys sticker, made our way into the place where boys become...well...less of being boys.

Alley-like the narrow venue smelled like every tattoo shop - Incense, tincture of green soap and rebellion. Though small, the place seemed adequately-equipped with vertical design displays, a customer counter, two chairs and a commode, not a restroom...just commode.

Being a Wednesday early-afternoon, there was only one other customer, a young woman, not hard to look at, dragging on a Marlboro red, having a red rose inked into her right, fully-exposed, breast. To avoid being splattered by the breast-work being done, her blouse was draped safely on the armchair to her left, leaving her completely topless.

Trying hard to look like *anything* but the eighteen year old late-bloomer I was, I pretended to "shop around", combing through the designs on display, hung vertically on a Rolodex-type gizmo like posters in a head shop, all the while knowing full-well the design I had in mind, as it was in my pants pocket. My cover was blown numerous times as I voyeuristically peered through the design rack, watching the work being done.

A one-man operation, the dude running the place, took a break from the rose job and welcomed me, asking how he could be of service. That's not exactly what he said. It was more Tommy Chong-like "What's up, man? - Look around – Check it out – Let me know what you're looking for and I'll get with ya when I'm done with this chick"

He was a real pro; shirtless as well, nipple rings, tatted head to toe, a loaded .45 in the back of his pants.

As he was talking, I wasn't intentionally avoiding eye contact I just hadn't stopped looking at them...her...as he chuckled kind of a stoned-like and remounted his stool, dipping his needle in the ink for another round.

She looked back at me, more in amusement I'm sure, but *why* mattered not to me; her look matured me by ten years. In the twinkling of her eye I was no kid anymore. Cut from the same cloth, her and me. Brother and sister from a different mister. I'd found my new home, my new people, so I took my rightful seat in the empty chair next to hers...I left my shirt on.

There was a soap opera on the 13 inch black and white in front of us. She lit another one as I tried to act uninterested in her top-lessness, watching the TV along with her, as the needle buzzed loudly, drowning out the volume on the TV.

"There ya go, my lady" he said, sitting back in admiration of his work. "Whatcha think...?" she cooed, as she turned them to-wards me.

Holy Mother of Jesus... "They're amazing..." *What are you saying, you dumb shit...* "...the pedals on your flowers..." *Oh my God!...Shut up!...Just stop talking!...*

She laughed, sexy-high-like, as she reached for her blouse, slipping it on, one arm at a time, reaching back...*Oh, I can't quite reach it...Could you help me...Ahhh...There...Got it,* I fantasized her saying.

Buttoning it slowly, intentionally, dropping me a look now and then. She put on quite a show.

I've got fifty bucks on me... I thought. I'd be back at the Christian Bookstore tomorrow, for the remission of my sins...but it'd be worth it.

"You ready, my man?" as I was rudely awakened from my fantasy.

"Hell ya!" as my voice cracked.

"Whatcha got there?" reaching for my sticker.

"Right on, man! -That's a *bad* mother fucker right there" Not sure if he meant the sticker or Jesus himself, but I agreed with both.

He free-handed the image onto my arm with a Bic ball-point pen. "Here we go, my bro" as he stabbed that needle twelve inches into my arm, it seemed. With the "chick" draggin' on another red just behind us I wouldn't, I couldn't, feel the pain. I tried to make small talk, like it was no big deal, as he dragged that hay hook through my right arm. In the weirdest way, before long the pain settled down, as did I.

In no time flat he said "Hey man, this is shaping up damn good... Let me put some color to it...You down with that?"

"Hell ya..." I said, in a now deeper voice.

Sitting back, wiping it down with the green soap, "Right on, man...Love it...Check it out..." he Chonged, as I stood leaning toward the mirror.

Still stinging a bit, but not bad, I loved it, not just the Ichthys and Jesus but what it stood for. I was in a tattoo shop in the hood of Houston getting tatted next to a topless chick by a guy with nipple rings and a .45 in his pants while Dad was lunching at the country club and Mom was leading Vacation Bible School at the church.

*Where's John? Has anyone seen John? Ya...He's down on Montrose getting a tattoo of a "bad mother fucker". That's where he's at...and he'll be home whenever he wants to be home...*I confidently said to myself, paying the dude and strutting outta that shop, like I owned the place.

That evening, at supper time, I strolled on into the kitchen with my newly-found swagger to join Mom and Dad for the evening meal.

"John! What's happened to your arm, honey", Mom empathetically asked, as she carefully rolled my t-shirt sleeve upward for a look. Dad looked on much differently, his expression more *pathetic* than *empathetic.* Though himself inkless, I'm sure he served with some guys in the Navy who bore the same bandages as I. I looked defiantly right at him as Mom undressed the "wound".

Like a fish jumping on a still pond, as the Ichthys broke the surface, Mom gasped "Oh, John..." All Dad said was "Mercy", disgustedly. "You know those things are permanent?" he rhetorically blurted.

"I sure hope so..." I said overconfidently. "...What I went through to get this I don't want to go through again!"

As Mom gently washed "Jesus", wiping his dried blood, patting him dry, Dad went on, really pissed-off-like, "Those things have to be surgically removed...Did you even think about that?"

"Why would I think about having something surgically removed that I just had drilled into my skin?" I quipped back. Not sure where that voice was coming from but it was coming out loud and proud.

"Mercy" he mumbled again, as he stood from his chair and left the kitchen. I'd ventured out of The Box...and he didn't like it one bit...As I watched him walk away, I can't say I felt so great about it either.

Mom comfortingly said "This means a lot to you...doesn't it?" "Yes, it does" I replied quietly as I watched Dad disappear into the back bedroom.

My grandmother loved it the most, never once lecturing me about tattoos, the Old Testament laws, surgical removal or any of that nonsense. It said "Jesus" and that was all that mattered to her.

Dad never mentioned it again - but there was no mistaking he hated it. The only thing worse than an ass-chewing from your authority figures, is being ignored by them. If "Mercy" couldn't do it, silence would, and did, so back in The Box I went, making sure to keep my shirt on while in his country club locker room.

If a criminal sketch artist would ask the victims to describe the perpetrator named John Hornsby, at that time of my life, they'd say he was a people-pleasing, codependent, risk-averse, quitter of anything requiring effort, drunk punk that got along with everyone, could fix anything and loved doing so, excuse-ready, blamed others kind of guy that depended on attention and could manipulate you to get it...in a million ways. Self-awareness would also rank high on that list.

Oh...they would also say he was nice to everyone, always helpful and went out his way to lend a hand. That's because he had to...but a few of the million ways he'd get what he needed from you.

The deeper into The Box I laid, and longer I laid there, the clearer the question became. *I can't lose my own soul...but I can dang sure lose my self...What does it profit me, John Hornsby, to gain the approval of my very own father...yet lose my very self in the process? There's only negative return on that investment...* but it was an investment I wasn't willing to divest in...just yet.

From the quiet distance I began to hear

John, my son, come to me...You're weary and heavy laden...In

*me you'll find rest for your soul...My yoke is easy and my bur-
den light*

BORN AGAIN

The ten years after Mom's passing were just plain weird. I had been "promoted" from a field assignment to business development within the company. I would later learn those "opportunities" were more about Dad than me. *That'll boost your self-esteem.* He'd gotten me the job in the first place, why not the promotions as well? *You'd been riding those coat tails your whole life...Why get off now?* I'd subconsciously ask myself.

My new "opportunity" had me wearing suits and ties to work and meeting with customers, many of whom knew Dad and often asked about him. *Would I ever be known as anything other than "Ed's son"?*

Both of our wonderful children were born during these years. They've turned out great, thanks be to their mother. Wonderful as they are, I've earmarked some of their inheritance for the counseling they'll need as they work through the Father-Trying-To-Find-Himself Syndrome I have already hereby given, bequeathed, and devised to them, per stirpes, prior to my demise.

Bombarded by the questions of mid-life "What's a husband supposed to be like?" "What does a good father act like?" "Should I strive to become a company vice president?" "Why don't I like the things other *real* men like?" "Why don't I care about our finances like other *real* men do?" "Will I ever stop thinking about sex every day?" "What if I'm not as conservative as people assume that I am?" "Who am I?" "What am I?" "Where am I?" "Why am I?" You know...typical stuff.

As my alcohol recovery work deepened, my spirituality heightened, creating a crossroad in my journey. At that crossroad, the question from my youth returned, *Is it profitable to gain my Father's approval and lose myself?* The answer was "No!"

Then and there I cried out, *I'm tired, God...so very tired...All my life it's been Who does he want me to be?, What do they need me to be?, What do I have to be? Shoulda, Oughtta, Better be...I can't do it anymore...I can't go on like this...I'm done...I know you as The Great I AM, but I don't know who I am!*

What I heard in reply would forever change my life. It was Ashley County Arkansas all the way, as if sitting next to me in that church pew:

Verily, verily I say unto thee, Except a man be born again, he cannot see the kingdom of God...Except a man be born of water and of the spirit...John, my son, let me born you again, to be the one I intended all along.

Answering a call to ministry (Read Ol' Joe – A Parable of Rust and Renewal) I made a list of authority figures I needed to inform about the change in my career trajectory. I put Dad way down on the list, not as a lower priority but as the one I was least excited about telling. I expected *Mercy*...

God, true God not religious God, and Jesus, authentic Jesus not close-minded fundamental bullshit Jesus, are different than any other authority figures I've ever known. He gives me mercy alright, but not disgustedly or as a way to keep me in line...just *mercy*.

With a newly found confidence, from a higher source, Dad moved up on the list and I scheduled a breakfast to inform him

I'd be leaving the company to pursue my seminary education and full-time ministry. By that time, I had two more tattoos that I didn't feel *led* to tell him about.

Likely just being nice, but I interpreted as control, Dad wanted to *host* our meeting. Accepting my invitation for breakfast and a conversation, he reserved a table at the 19th hole at his country club for us to meet; always on his turf. I arrived early, to impress. *"Late people were lazy"*.

Like tattoo shops, all 19th holes smell about the same, like freshly mowed grass, prime rib, popcorn and mildew. Small-talk and chit-chat, we made our way through our first cup, but I knew who I was dealing with and wasted no time in getting to it.

As the waitress, he knew by name, topped off our coffee, "Dad, you know I've been wrestling around with my career and... uhhh..." twirling my spoon "...it's been tough...for a while now...trying to figure it all out...and ...uhhhh..." *Is this the right move?* "...I've been doing lots of thinking and soul-searching... and Kim and I feel strongly about a calling to...uhhhh..." *Did he even like Grand Daddy?* "...going full-time into ministry...so... uhhh..."

Looking straight at me, not over me or through me, but into me he said "John, I've never been more proud of you".

What's happening right now?

"All your mother and I ever wanted for the three of you is for you to be happy and find yourselves - Sounds like you've done just that."

Mom's name-drop, accepted...

He continued, "I'm gonna help with your house payment for a while until all this shakes out for you"

Not sure how I feel about this...

"That kind of work doesn't pay much and the road could get rocky. I want to help Kim and the kiddos stay in your good neighborhood, stay with their friends and in their good schools"

What I heard was *You can't do this without my help.*

Was this a blessing? - I couldn't tell. You can't take care of yourself? - Probably

What I *did* know was that my prepared defensive replies were left in my saddlebag, un-needed, as he surprisingly approved of my course correction.

"Thank you" as our plates were cleared from the table. I'm sure we talked a bit more, but probably not much more. When *he* was done, *we* were done. Torn between competing emotions, relishing that he'd approved of my decision yet feeling like a charity-case, dependent, little boy...yet again, I didn't say much after that, only "...Ya, I'm starting to look at seminaries...Pretty exciting..."

Dad's love language to us was "Provider" and he did that so very well. Meanwhile, he handicapped the Hell out of me; I knew not how to neither fight nor fail; I'd never had to do either.

Although I'd answered the highest of callings, well above even Dad, in my deep need to be close to him, I accepted Dad's offer– because, again, that's what I do.

MERLE

Years had gone by since that breakfast conversation; I'd attended one seminary for years before discovering I didn't "fit-in" with that fundamental, apologist-wannabe crowd there, transferring to and graduating from a different seminary, where I "fit-in", at least, better. I ended up teaching at that seminary for a couple of years after graduation. There's some really good folks there.

I'd done a lot of supply preaching in and around the area, only to discover I didn't "fit-in" with the suit-wearing, pantyhose-fitted preacher/wife crowd (Kim wore the pantyhose, not me). I love them and need them to equip me for my ministry, but I'm not one of them.

Assuming all along I'd be a preacher of some sort, I found I was more of a pastor than preacher, caring for grieving souls as they travelled along the rocky road of life, sometimes in the here and now, other times on their way to the ever-after. I found that I didn't "fit-in" anywhere per se.

As badly as I needed to "fit-in" and be accepted somewhere, the more I didn't "fit-in" anywhere. I wasn't a rodeo pro, still can't surf, quit baseball, quit drinking, put down the guitar, and quit preaching. Honestly I began to feel alone....not lonely, but alone.

Jesus had said once:

Foxes have holes, and birds of the air have nests; but the son of man hath not where to lay his head.

Luke 9:58

As I'd walk and talk with Jesus, I'd here *John, my brother, I feel ya... I don't fit in anywhere either....my own family doesn't understand me...The synagogue doesn't know what to do with me...The religious nuts have had enough of me...I really have no place to lay my head... no place to call "home"...You might feel alone out here, but you'll never be lonely...I'm always with you...*

For me, it usually happens this way; when I hit a crossroad, Jesus shows up. He drove up this time in the hot rod I'd never had.

Emptying our nest, as it's called, with both kids grown, on their own and outta the house, Kim and I were adjusting to this new chapter in our lives. By God's grace we'd kept the fire going in our relationship so we didn't suffer from "Who the Hell are you? Syndrome" as some empty nesters do when their kids are gone.

Kim remained at our old church, teaching kids in pre-K; she's amazing there. Ministry/work was going well for me, as I was cutting more and more of my own path, yet continuing to "Silence the Lambs" of the omnipotent approver-of-a-voice in my head. He just wouldn't shut up...or I just kept listening...

I'd already put my therapist's two kids through college, working through this, yet remnants of The Box remained.

Ten years, and three boring sedans, after Ol' Joe left us, Hank randomly asked me "Hey, man, it's been a long time. Ever wanna do another Ol' Joe or something? You don't have much going on these days" (Funny their impression of our life after they fly the coup).

"Maybe..." I said, pondering...

"Cool. What would ya get?"

Without hesitation, "'68 to '72 Olds Cutlass, sport coupe, two-door hard top,"

"Daaannnggg, that didn't take long…What's up with a Cutlass?"

"Takes me back…" as it did while I was saying that.

"…to a time…to a place I like to revisit now and then…" I replied trance-like.

Looking at me inquisitively, "Where you at, Dad?"

"Heading to Little League practice…Seat belt buckle just blistered me…Vinyl seats're doing the same…Ronnie Milsap's on KIKK radio…Copenhagen's tucked in my sock, hidden up my pant leg…Mom's driving…"

Mom didn't even pursue a driver license until she and Dad married, but then drove a lot of cool cars. She had the '64 Impala I pin-striped red with a spray can of Krylon, and the sweet '68 Mustang we still miss, the '71 Buick Skylark Cristy and I nose-dived and totaled, a '72 Mustang, '76 Olds Cutlass that I joy-drove, under-age, to the tune of about ten thousand miles. Used to "flip the breather" on that Cutlass; sounded cooler that way.

After that Cutlass, her cool cars became much less cool, starting with her first of many Buick Regals. Dad must've had something for the Buick lot, because he started buying all her cars from there; used and new. The dealership was probably run by some fraternal friend of Dad's from a club he belonged to.

You mention one idea, a thought, a passing notion, to Hank and he is on it like white on rice. Before I finished telling him where it took me, he had found a selection of '68 to '72 Cutlasses on his iPhone for us to consider, although I wasn't "considering" any-thing…until he asked. Once I saw the pictures online, I knew I shouldn't have looked.

Like an alcoholic dodging the beer joint or a diabetic ditching a donut shop, I knew better than to even sneak a peek at the pictures. Like AA taught me *If you keep going to the barbershop, you're gonna wind up with a haircut.* I did and before I knew it I was in the chair, shears just a humming.

Having warned Hank that we weren't exactly bathing in Benjamins (I mean our restoration budget dictates "The Deader the Better") he found some affordable ones and we began making a few calls.

Lamar, that's what we'll call him, because that's his name, confirmed that his Cutlass was still on the market and we arranged a look-see later that afternoon.

'Twas the holiday season so the whole fam-damily was in town and, with no child left behind, we loaded up to check out this Cutlass all together. Donning my Ol' Joe baseball shirt, the crew made the trek south of town and met Lamar and his Uncle Benny. Taking us around back, there she was, beside Uncle Benny's wood-sided garage where he was tinkering with a '52 Chevy pick-up.

The Cutlass had been in its place since the early nineties, with promise after broken promise to someday be restored. Lamar needed cash, and we wanted a project, so our timing was nothing short of divine.

There was little doubt that it'd been there a good while; flat tires, rusted dash, torn up upholstery, a rodent road-show, with rat's nests and half-eaten pecan hulls galore. Pleasantly surprised after pulling the hood latch, there was an Oldsmobile Rocket 350, fully intact, but moaned *"20 years-worth of uncranked"*.

Body was in pretty good shape, considering, and all the vitals were there. I was thinking *Maybe we got something to work with.*

Despite the rat crap, dirt, debris and pecan hulls I broke the seal, opening the driver's door and took a seat, as the moisture of the split-bench seat crept through my jeans and wetted my backside. Made no matter to me...The cool moisture soothed the hot, seat vinyl in my soul...

Her style, the vibe she put off, took me where I'd wanted to go for a long time...*where I needed to go...*

My increasing *need* for the car did nothing to increase the *cash* in my pocket, so I tried to play it cool...as you're supposed to do in times like that. I guess it worked, plus Lamar was a great guy, because we settled on a fair price right away and I made arrangements for a flat-bed haul truck to meet us back there a couple of hours later to take her home.

Leaving Lamar's I had to laugh at myself. How could I think I had room to negotiate when my entire family, including mother-in-law, came to the car deal? He saw me coming before I was even headed his way.

With the crew we brought along, it took two cars to get us all there. Leaving the neighborhood we got separated for a short time as Kim and her Mother were held up at the stop sign until the drug deal in front of them was done. Amazon Prime doesn't hold a candle to the delivery speed of the kid running out to that car.

Arriving back at Lamar's, the Cutlass was already in front of the house, in perfect position to be loaded. Asking Lamar how he got the tires aired and the car rolled out so quickly he replied "'Roun' heya we gets by widda lil hep from our friends, if ya knows what I mean" - I did.

As we awaited Tony, the haul truck driver, to arrive, Lamar popped the trunk and showed me the new parts he'd already purchased but hadn't yet installed; water pump, thermostat and a few other things; nothing major but nice to have and nice for him to offer. Tony arrived and the Cutlass was northbound in no time flat.

Being the holidays, and a bit cold out, the neighborhood was much quieter than when Ol' Joe had been hauled in. The Cutlass would slip in without a lot of fanfare. The few folks that *were* out gave their approval with a thumbs-up and *Oh, here he goes again* smiles. The rest of them just nodded as if *I wish my wife loved old hot rods like his does...*

Tony was a maneuvering maestro and had that Cutlass up my sloped driveway and slid safely into her garage bay, the exact same spot where Ol' Joe had been landed almost 20 years before.

High-fiving and settling up with Tony, he went on his way, off to make another old man's dreams come true...or take him back to his childhood...

Walking around her, she truly was the hot rod I'd always wanted but never had. The deader the better was revealing her true self; there was a lot of work to do...but it's the *work* we love doing.

Hood up, we tore into her, assessing what had to go and what was worth hanging onto. Typical tear-down, we drained her, flushed her and filled her with fresh fluids head-to-toe. Her little two-barrel got an overhaul, along with new plugs, wires and battery; funny what comes to life when connected to the source. Her headlights still worked, even some of her dash lights. As I inserted the square-headed brass ignition key her door buzzed. Cracked us up...and gave us hope.

"What-da-we-got-to lose?" I said as Hank and I prepared to give her a crank. "Here goes" as I turned that well-worn, brass key. She turned over...We did as well. Hank hit her rebuilt carb with some starter fluid and we tried again. She fired, sputtered and died. Smelling gas, I hit it again and she fired up and idled rough, but ran until we cut her off. Checking for leaks, we found none, right away. Starting her once more we let her idle for a few minutes until "Shut 'er down, Dad!" Hank hollered from under the hood. As I peered under her raised hood, the radiator spewed and sprayed all over the place. Time had eaten away and corroded her, perforating her skin. She was about as tight as a moth-eaten sweater.

San Antonio summers can get the best of you, and your radiator, so we ordered a desert cooler and banged out enough space for a snug, but good fit. Once in place, she was good to go and "cool" as she could be.

Typical road worthiness work like wheel bearings, hubs, brakes, brake lines, shocks and, of course, wheels and tires and she was ready for a road test.

Our garage, being at the peak of a sloped driveway, was a place we needed be able to get back into once out and about, so we made sure she had power in both directions, Drive and Reverse; best we could tell both worked.

With Hank behind me and a scrap lumber 4 x 4 wheel chock in-hand, in case she got away from us, I eased backwards down the driveway. New brakes worked just fine. Once in the street, I slipped her into Drive and she lunged forward, a good start. She and I idled around the cul-de-sac just fine, but she had trouble whenever I'd put any kind of load on her; not engine trouble but tranny trouble.

With her tranny slipping bad, we pushed, shoved, moaned and begged her back into the garage. More work to be done.

Yes, there was transmission fluid. From what we could tell, everything was in place and connected. Hank's YouTube research suggested a rebuild kit. Over-confidently I ordered one, along with the manual. A few evenings later Hank and I would dive into the worse decision we'd made in a long time.

Being a typical two-bay, suburban neighborhood garage we had no hydraulic lift or anything of the sort. I bought some high and heavy-duty jack stands and we lifted her as high as we safely could, and as high as necessary to pull her tranny, and begin the bench rebuild.

Feeling about as secure as we could we crawled underneath and began to pull the transmission; wasn't difficult at all. Resting it on a floor jack and rolling it out sideways, we were in business.

An old friend of mine's Dad owned a transmission shop in east

Houston years ago, but was now retired. He offered to counsel me on the rebuild. I talked to him "It's a little turbo 350...If you're gonna break out on one, that's the one to do it on...Any fool can do one of those..." Apparently not *any* fool.

I'd cleared the bench and she was laying on the gurney ready for surgery. Manual in-hand and YouTube on standby we began the disassembly. As Hank got about as far as the valve body, I got about as far as pouring the rebuild kit from the box. We looked at each other, as the YouTube guy talked in a language we couldn't understand, and, without saying a word, we poured the parts back in the box, lifted the tranny into a cardboard box and slid it into the bed of my truck. I'd take it to a shop the next day for a rebuild estimate. Brain surgeons don't hold a candle to transmission rebuilders. We were *way* out of our league.

The estimates to rebuild were higher than the rebuilt ones on-line that already had shift kits. No-brainer. I got $40 for the aluminum housing at the recycle center and our new transmission would arrive in a week or two. Our decisions were getting better and better.

Back underneath, new tranny on the floor jack, we rolled it in place and hooked her up. Easiest thing we'd done for a while. Fluid full we took her for a drive. A smooth shifting tranny had never felt so good.

Kim and I made the actual maiden voyage, like we always have. About 11:30 one night we loaded up and went for a drive. Without seats, I sat on a 5-gallon bucket as a driver's seat. Kim rolled towels and blankets as a passenger seat, holding her feet up because the floor pans were non-existent, and off we went.

Rounding the block I smiled at her as the new tranny shifted smoothly from first to second to third, downshifting on her own when necessary. *Why not go one more lap?* We thought to ourselves...

Backside of our neighborhood, she quit, leaving us to coast up against the curb. Cranking on her a few times, she wasn't firing at all, so I guessed gas.

Leaving Kim in the dark, on her blankets and towels, curbside in the back of our neighborhood, I ran home for the little red gas can, the same one Ol' Joe had left with us.

Returning as fast as my well-worn, black, low-top Chucks would get me, I put the two gallons in her. She fired immediately and we put her up for the night. Kim's such a sweetheart. Although she might have been thinking it, but I doubt it, she never once said *What a dumbass I married...Does he ever get anything right?* She's always right there beside me, unconditionally. She's mine so back off.

You know, I sit and wonder sometimes about women like Kim and Mom. They're special and the world could use more good folks like 'em; selfless, behind-the-scenes, believe in you more than you believe in yourself. They just make you better by being around 'em. The Cutlass was like that too. There was something special about being out in the garage with her; I was better by being around her.

In the late seventies, early eighties, the wrench turners and gear heads I knew built and drove muscle cars - Camaro, GTO, Chevelle, Mustang, Firebird (Trans Am for rich kids who drove 'em but didn't build 'em), Road Runner, Cuda, and such.

The Jeff Spicolis (a.k.a. "heads and waste-o's") drove Monte Carlos and Gran Torinos. Bud Davis-types (a.k.a. Urban Cowboys and Kickers like me) drove trucks, two-door trucks with gun racks and picnic (or Pizza Hut) tablecloth curtains in the rear windshield, with fuzzy dingle balls stitched on the fringe. No wonder I now wanted a hot rod...and, now I had one. She was meek but muscled, a beauty with some beast, southern charm and a warm hug, but could run your ass back to the house if you needed it, shrewd as a serpent and gentle as a dove, a bodhisattva of sorts, a psychopomp to guide my soul onward– exactly what I'd been looking for – I named her "Merle".

EST. 1926

Merle Cloteen Sparks was born the middle child to an Arkansas couple; a logging man and a dedicated wife. Called into The Gospel Ministry, mid-life (sounds familiar) they relocated their young family to Texas and began serving their calling in various churches.

As my uncle would recently tell me, while pastoring a small Baptist church in Luling, Texas, Grand Daddy would go out, mid-week, into the oil fields and minister to the roughnecks and roustabouts. One Saturday afternoon he baptized 60 of them in the San Marcos River. Tells me where I got the bug for the working folks.

Clo Hornsby was a role model for a lot of things, way beyond homemaker, mother and wife. She incarnated someone much higher in the pecking order than June Cleaver; she brought Jesus to life each day through the way she *loved her neighbor as herself*. Guess her Daddy's sermons hit home. Faith and works were one and the same in the abbreviated life of Clo Hornsby. The world was a better place while she was here.

Mom and Dad were both raised Southern Baptist, but you would only know that because Dad wouldn't drink around their church friends, except those church friends who also didn't drink around their church friends. It was full-time job for him remembering what image he had to keep up on any given day, at any given time.

We were in church every Sunday morning, Sunday evening and Wednesday night prayer meeting, doing Sunday School, Training Union, choir, RAs, GAs, church basketball, the whole enchilada. Some of my fondest memories of Mom are in church.

Oftentimes, about the third point too many of a long-ass, boring sermon, I'd look up at her with my sleepy eyes and she'd look back at me, smiling the way only she could, lips downwardly curved, empathetic, loving, compassionate, letting me know I am loved, with just her smile. There was no way Jesus could love me any more than that...no matter what the preacher said or the Good Book told me.

Mom's faith colored beautifully outside the lines of tradition and religion, but never in a way to offend or make a statement. She simply let Jesus do his thing in her and through her. Make a note of that.

One sleepy afternoon at the church house, a young John Denver-looking guy showed up, in his Ford Falcon that had broken down, barely making it into the parking lot. His faithful, loyal companion, an elderly basset hound, slept underneath the car, with water bowl nearby.

As the nursery department staff meeting let out, Mom met the young man, introduced herself and asked to hear his story. He'd come from California, heading to I can't remember where and landed in our church parking lot, unable to move on with a broke-down Falcon. Mom's faith and works came together.

Home from work, Dad was greeted by *three* of us; mom, me and the John Denver look-a-like. Dad wasn't pleased. Dad was a man of faith, taught Sunday School, served on the finance committee and all that but was not cool with this shirtless drifter being in our house.

There was a *brief* couple's conference in the Kitchen. Mom did the talking and Dad did the listening...I did the eavesdropping.

Subsequent to their conversation, the young man not only stayed for supper but spent the night with us.

Raymond, the local mechanic, was called and asked to go by and fix the young man's car the next morning. Dad still didn't like it, but we often don't like what Jesus tells us to do. He'd heard from Jesus in the kitchen and he wasn't arguing any longer. If there was one person Ed Hornsby wouldn't argue with, it was Jesus... and he'd been married to her long enough to know better.

"We wear shirts at our supper table" Dad grunted at him, letting him know he wasn't welcome, as if the guy couldn't already tell.

"Then go get him one out of Paul's closet" came that Arkansas sweet tea voice from the kitchen. Like a rebellious teenager being made to do what his mother told him, Dad reluctantly stomped off down the hallway to fetch the required, supper table shirt.

"Here. Put this on...and we don't want it back", he said, tossing the shirt in the general direction of the drifter. *Being Jesus is tough...Living with her is even tougher.*

After supper, the table was cleared. The drifter did the dishes. We then retreated to the den for more conversation. He asked if ok to smoke. Mom said "yes" in unison with Dad who said "No". Dad smoked pipes and cigars all the time inside...but he wasn't a homeless drifter. He rolled his own with some Bugler and a Zig Zag, as Mom brought him the ashtray from the coffee table. *So, we do smoke in the house...*

He asked if we liked music. Mom said "We sure do". Dad didn't hear the question, still huffing about the smoking stranger. He returned from the guest bedroom with a small black case and opened it beside the couch/sofa, tapping his ashes into the ash tray. He then pulled a beautiful trumpet from his case and wet his lips. He blew beautiful music.

That generation loved brass music and Dad was a sucker for it; Doc Severinsen, The Nashville Brass and the infamous Pete

Fountain, Dad's favorite. When the young man began "Just a Closer Walk with Thee" Dad's countenance changed, his face softening, as if the drifter guided him now on a "...Closer Walk..." The song mellowed him like a good scotch.

Mom looked at Dad and smiled; that same smile I saw in the church pew. She knew Dad loved that song. The drifter blew something special through that horn of his, something Dad needed in that moment.

I'm sure Dad still slept with one eye open, but, the next morning, after Raymond got the young man's car started, Dad gave him some cash and wished him well. Mom prayed over him and sent him back down the road to wherever, without a doubt glad he had broken down at Clo Hornsby's church.

On my 19th birthday, the summer before my sophomore year in college, some good friends of mine took me out for a night on the town. The night began with dinner at my folks' house, including one of Mom's wonderful, scratch-made meals, like only she could make. There were about five or six of us there, along with Mom and Dad. Dinner was served in the formal dining room, just off the kitchen with the two louvered doors that separated the two areas.

Back then 19 was the legal drinking age. The year before, on my 18th, besides getting my first tattoo, I enjoyed liquor legality for 11 days until the privilege was stripped from me, at least the "legal" privilege. No law had stopped me, or even slowed me down, my freshman year in college.

Before all 19 candles were lit on my cake the doorbell chimed unexpectedly. Wondering who'd be coming by that time of the evening, my birthday buddies all looked expectantly at me, letting me know I was the one to answer the door. We had a party night already planned, commencing after we left my parents' house...but the party would begin much sooner.

Opening the front door of our quietly cul-de-sac'd, upscale, sub-urban house, the home that Clo and Ed Hornsby dreamed of in their premarital love letters, where, at birth I was carried through the very front door I was now answering, to be nursed by my Mother, the very Mother who'd made this special evening so very special – That's the front door I opened - and where I was greeted by a girl whom I had not yet met but would soon know better than I could have imagined.

She waited *not* for permission to enter our residence, but came on in. Dressed in an overcoat, derby-style hat and carry bag she made her way to our dining room table, introducing herself, briefly before losing the overcoat, as we lost our minds. What are friends for? They had arranged a stripper for the evening and had her come to my parents' house during dinner in our formal dining room.

The carry bag she toted unzipped and out came her cassette tape player, jamming some disco song as she replaced the derby hat with a pair of white, furry bunny ears. The show had begun...and oh what a show it was. Ever been caught between the two worlds you live in? I came-to, mid-dance, to remember this wasn't going down in a club with my college buddies, but in my parents' dining room. They weren't away from home travel-ing for business, as they often did; they were center-stage.

Looking at my buddies as if *I'm gonna kill all of you later...but thanks!* I then looked at Dad. He seemed to be having a grand time with this portion of the program. As I hesitantly turned toward Mom a flash bulb exploded in my would-soon-be-red pupils.

From behind her Kodak Instamatic, there she was...smiling ear-to-ear taking picture after picture. Frame by frame she slipped further from her little, white-steepled, clap-boarded, stained glass upbringing. Watching Mom in that moment, I saw an ex-hibition of unconditional love and grace rarely seen by anyone claiming to follow Jesus. Mom wasn't lost in the *lasciviousness* of it; she was loved the girl...just as Jesus does.

Those pictures, the select ones, were proudly displayed in our family photo album which Mom updated throughout our childhood and early adult life. She had developed a lot more pictures than showed up in the album. Never saw those. Dad must've kept them somewhere safe.

She then did what Clo Hornsby did so well. The disco died down and the dance was over. Cottontail finished her show and prepared to exit...but that didn't happen. Mom invited her to join us at the table, making her a plate and a piece of cake, insisting she join us for the candle lighting that was about to resume. I barely had the breath to blow out the candles...and the wish I made was much different than before the doorbell rang.

The young woman really settled in and seemed to enjoy hanging out with our family and friends. Mom never tried to "lead her to Jesus" or "convict her of her sins"; she just loved her and included her. No doubt the girl enjoyed the meal, and I'm sure waited for the string attached. No such string; just love.

While performing, strippers have to protect themselves from being touched. No doubt that young woman was *touched* at our house, touched by the Spirit in Clo Hornsby. She had that effect on everyone she met.

It's too rare an occasion we find stereo-typical Christians anywhere near people like this, but Jesus hung out with them all the time, by going to their place! There, he ate with them, listened to them, didn't preach at them, and loved them, purely and unconditionally. The first-century followers of Jesus saw it first-hand. What a privilege it must've been for them, seeing God in the flesh. And, for 60 years, a few of us had the privilege of seeing God in the flesh, first-hand, in the life of Clo Hornsby.

HOME

A million miles from yesterday and a million more to go

Still I search each day

Trying to find my way home

Gov't Mule

They say a smell can take you somewhere faster than any of the other senses. Cedar, pipe tobacco and green beans with slivered almonds and I'm at the Hunters' house. Manure and rosin and I'm behind the bucking chutes. The drawer lining of antique furniture takes me to Cristy. Diesel exhaust? I'm shredding pastures at the ranch. Surf wax and incense and I'm with Paul. Copenhagen puts me in a treehouse at Lake Travis looking at Playboy centerfolds, the first whiff from the popped top on a Budweiser still makes my mouth water and the brittle pages of old hymnals and Bibles put me in the pew, next to Mom.

I love old churches; not their religion, but where they take me and whom I meet there. The aroma of oiled wood bannisters, creepy-feeling velvety-cushioned pews, musty and communion wine-spotted carpet, blended with the ever-present scent of percolated coffee from the fellowship hall and I'm there, sword drawn and ready for the invitation. There's something/

someone there.

Most people, including yours truly, are repulsed by the oldness of antiquated churches and their judgement, fire and brimstone, and rightfully so. But beneath all that debris, buried under the pew cushions, inserted between the pages of old Bibles, lying dormant within the scriptures...is the authentic Jesus; that's who I meet there.

In similar fashion, as the thumb pushbutton depressed and I opened Merle's driver's door in Lamar's backyard, the smell hit me - The sweet aroma of the unborn, a soon-to-be-restored vintage car. It's gotta be the decaying synthetic fabrics in the carpet, headliner and upholstery. Wherever it stems from it creates a smell that takes you back – to sideburns, white t-shirts, Brylcreem and a gal beside you with a fresh beehive hairdo, scarf and cat-eye sunglasses. I can still see Mom in hers.

After getting Merle to my garage, as an extension of my home pest control, I began stripping out all that old fabric, headliner, carpet, seats, and door panels, anything that could be removed from that Fisher Body trim package. As each panel came off, the aroma transitioned from "Those were the days..." to..."...rat shit", which took me back to nowhere, except the trash can and out to the curb.

I've had an interest, allure, borderline fascination, with my childhood for as long as I can remember, and just being around this '71 Olds Cutlass, sport coupe, two-door hardtop I'd named Merle was driving me there in record time.

Our old house at 5830 Picasso - I knew every square inch of it. The neighborhood - I'd ridden my bike up and down every street and knew every expansion joint, driveway, vacant lot, side yard, drainage ditch and back alley within a few square miles of my house. I could ride it, run it, skateboard it, unicycle it, even drive it home drunk...all with my eyes closed, and sometimes did.

My old schools and the memories made there, the yards I mowed, the pranks I pulled, the trouble I caused, the highs and lows of childhood, death and suicide around the neighborhood, returning Vietnam veterans, all of that is tattooed more deeply than in my flesh. There was something back there that wanted my attention…and Merle was getting me there.

A few months after Merle made it to my garage I was back in Houston for a morning meeting and dinner engagement. Having a lengthy afternoon break, I made good use of my time and returned to the hood for a drive-thru. Passing the old church, I exited Hillcroft and pulled into the parking lot, parking right about the same spot where the drifter had broken down, more than four decades before.

On a whim, I entered the church office, welcomed by the Southern Baptist committee of coffee and sugar cookie smells from down the hall, and checked in with the receptionist. Nice lady, looked the part, accommodating and welcoming, unlike a few church staffers I've met, but appropriately cautious of my wanting to be there.

Introducing myself, surely she'd know the name (arrogant ass I am), I asked if I could "just walk around and reminisce a bit", telling her I'd remain in the sanctuary and main lobby areas. After giving her my driver license she agreed and off I went. The last time I'd left that office I had dropped off an apology letter Mom made me write for being "dismissed" from the Christian Sex Education Class offered to our youth group. I'd rather not say why.

Although the old sanctuary had been converted into a children's wing, the newer sanctuary still took me where I wanted to go. I was in high school when that new sanctuary was built and I recalled *precious memories, how they linger*, of my teenage years as I walked pew by pew up and down the aisles. It felt really, really good in there - Quiet, illuminated only by the floor-to-ceiling stained glass windows; Jesus, some lambs, apostles, cross, typical church glass.

The pipe organ, the main selling point of the building fund, still presented itself majestically above the multi-tiered choir loft, where the antique white with green neck-sashed choir would belt "Up from the grave he arose!" when a new believer would surface from their immersion. As I reminiscently relived those good times, standing silently in the center aisle just in front of the Lord's Supper table, I was brought back to the present by "Uhhh...Hello?...May I help you?"

"Oh...hey there...I'm John Hornsby...(Enough with the arrogance) I used to go here as a kid and...uhhh...just felt led to come by and... check it out...It's a cool place...and ...uhhh...feels good in here..." as I looked beyond the young man...upward toward the baptistry.

"Cool, man. I'm the music minister and we have a lot of elderly families still with us that were probably here when you and your folks were members" As he rattled off a few hall of famers, whose names I knew well, the memories became even more precious.

Thanking him, I benedictioned my way back out the center aisle and returned to the Church office, where I was greeted by the now-smiling receptionist as she handed me a good-sized paperback magazine-looking thing, open to a specific page. It was the Church Directory from 1971 and our family's picture was post-it marked. She'd dug this thing out of the archives as I toured the place. It was the family photo Dad had on his office credenza, as required.

Smiling, as if saying *I know this will mean a lot to you,* she handed me the directory; our picture said it all. Mom was picture-perfect and Church Directory-appropriate. Dad looked like he'd come from a contract negotiation. He dressed the same for church as he did for work; says a lot.

Cristy, and her new hairdoed self, stood behind Mom, looking as if she hoped Dad approved of her new "do". Paul nonchalantly stood behind Dad, butt-cut surfer-long hair, side burns, his facial expression like he didn't give a shit – 'cause he *didn't*.

And, there, nestled safely next to Mom, sat me...dressed like a *good boy* should, smiling as I had learned to do, internally knowing I *was* the wussy I looked like. *Was that mother's milk on my shirt collar?* The receptionist was much more impressed by the photo than I.

After seeing enough, I folded it closed, returning it to and thanking her for her hospitality. I inhaled deeply, just once more, the Spirit there, and left.

Having not yet checked into my hotel, my overnight bag was in the trunk of my rented sedan. My running shoes, shorts and a t-shirt came along on this trip in case I "felt the urge" for a run. I suddenly *felt the urge*.

Rolling together my gear, I made my way into the church gym to change in the locker room. No receptionist there. This was the same gymnasium, as we called it, where I'd spent many a summer morning playing dodgeball and many an evening on the church basketball team, the league where parents got to act un-Jesus-like for one night a week.

Changing quickly, I placed my dress clothes back in the trunk, stretched out a bit and began a slow jog out of the parking lot. I'd return a couple of hours later.

The smell of chlorine drew my nostrils toward Maplewood swimming pool, just across the street from the church. Rounding the perimeter fence and parking lot, although closed for the season, I could still hear KRBE blasting from the outdoor speaker, lifeguard whistles and "Adult Swim". There's the low board where I never mastered the gainer...and the high dive where a "can opener" was the best I could do, hoping to splash the hot-chick lifeguard who cared *not* that I existed.

Onward, down the block I jogged. The tree branches arched

over the concrete street (we'd never heard of asphalt). Cicadas buzzed cyclically and deafeningly loud. The houses were vintage 60's, ranch-style Americana, wood-shingled, many had the built-in bird houses up in their gable. Now and then you might see remnants of an actual nest poking from one of the holes, but rarely.

Crossing Chimney Rock, then over the drainage ditch footbridge, where I saw my first drug deal; one "Head" to another, I then made my way around the chain link fence of Johnston Junior High, past the outdoor courts, football field and track. Around Willowbend, once by the main entrance, I was drawn in, unable to resist the urge...So I went inside.

After-school practices were going on and the janitorial staff didn't seem to care that a sweaty, grown man in gym shorts, a complete stranger, walked through the halls in the late afternoon (Never big on security). The last time I'd walked those halls I was in a pair of high-top Chuck Taylors and sweaty gym shorts, those uniform blue ones with a white stripe down the side. They always smelled like mildew...at least mine did.

Albert Sidney Johnston and I had split the sheets the spring of '78 and I hadn't been back, but nothing had changed except everything was smaller than I remembered, or maybe I was just bigger.

Slowly, I walked the ever-long, locker-lined hallways of that old school. It smelled exactly the same, like Stridex medicated pads, cartridge pens and the essence of pubescence. White butcher paper lined the walls with cheerleader-speak for the football team to "Beat 'em Bust 'em", whomever 'em was.

There's the class where I failed science... and stairwell where I didn't make it to the boys' room (nerves and chili). From a good ways off I began to hear the dribbling basketballs and coaches' whistles; I was close to the gym.

Sidelined just inside the doorway, I saw the basketball court (just like Hoosiers), even more yellowed and worn than before, with its painted lines marking the down and backs we ran, horse after horse, during tryouts. I ran them in Levis blue jeans, bare-footed…and beat every kid there. I'd just heard that afternoon there were tryouts. I'm sure there were announcement flyers posted around the school, or the coaches probably told us during gym class, but I never paid any attention to any of that…or anyone. I lived in in my own little world.

The other kids showed up prepared, with gym bags, extra clothes and all that. I just showed up – and outran 'em all, catching the coach's eye. "Who wants to race him now!" he'd yell. Doubled over and gasping after their last horse, no one else stepped up. I re-socked my bare feet and slid back into my Tony Lamas and rode my bike home. I made a couple of more of the tryouts, but when it came to actual basketball skills I quit showing up, making up lame excuse after lame excuse, and finally was cut, simply for not showing up. I lied to Dad about it and told him "I tried my hardest…and…just don't know what happened". I was a fearful quitter. That's what had happened.

There's the courtyard, where the "courting" took place. At least it did on dance nights; had my first kiss there. Today that girl is in a beautiful, same-sex relationship and very happy. Makes me smile – to think I must've kissed like a girl - and she liked it.

Back on the street, again catching my stride, I jogged down Chimney Rock, blowing a bit at the stop light before crossing over and landing on the street-level, grassy ridge of Braes Bayou. Peering down into that bayou, my soul revived with every breath of fresh cut grass, cool and damp from the humidity, and the memories upon memories down in that glamorous ditch.

Braes Bayou, at its normal flow, was but a three-foot wide waterway and had wide concrete flats that sloped upward about twenty feet creating a cement curl that we skateboarders could ride for miles after dropping in off the grassy edge. That bayou was a winding way that I'd been up and down my entire childhood. Running on, my pace picked up as I neared home.

Another mile or so, past the Jewish Community Center and Beth Israel, "Hear, O Israel; the Lord our God is one Lord..." turning left, then right then left again I arrived – at Picasso Place.

Stopping at the corner, catching my breath, I began a slow walk past every yard I'd mowed... every door I'd ding-dong-ditched...every Arizona Ash and Cottonwood I'd climbed. Still in the paved street was every splatter of concrete spilled when they first poured it back in the early '60s; still there, right where I'd left them. My parents were my age when they moved from Picasso to Dallas. Now, here I was, back there yet again, looking for what I'd left behind.

Stopping in front of 5830 Picasso Place, I needed to further catch my breath, from the run and the exhilaration of being back on Picasso. The "For Sale" sign in the yard, with accompanying lock box on the door handle and carless driveway, suggested it might be empty. Breaking and entering wasn't an option so I walked the sidewalk, with a false sense of ownership to the place. It was no longer mine, yet something inside the house was. Giving the front door a knock – the five-rap knock I've used my whole life, I then waited...

Brief silence – *Maybe it's empty after all* - The deadbolt clacked and the door opened slowly - a man peering cautiously from behind it, leaning forward just enough to see me – his wife standing in the background, in full view.

"Hello...You don't know me, but I was born and grew up in this house, many years ago...I don't want to come in...just jogging the old neighborhood and couldn't resist coming by"

Eyebrow raised in further suspicion - "Is that right?" long pause, looking me up and down, his motionless wife frozen, still in full view. "The back bedroom looks like an add-on. Is it?" he tested me.

"Yes...We added it in the early 70's when my grandmother came to live with us. She lived here until she died, then I lived back there...There was a false wall in the closet in there, built to store Dad's guns and hunting gear...Didn't know if you knew that or not"

Stepping from behind the door, now also in full view, he went on "Ohhhhh, so that's why it was configured that way. We had it remodeled years ago, converting it into one giant closet for my wife and we wondered what it was for"

His chit-chatter fell on deaf ears as I fixated on the serving counter that joined the kitchen and den. He and his wife now at the door, they went on and on about the house and how they'd loved it, as their voices faded into the distance. Mom was behind that serving counter, apron around her hips, silk bloused, sleeves rolled, hands white with flour, Crisco and the mixer to her right, looking right at me, smiling that smile that said *I love you so, my dear little boy, and have missed you. I know the burdens you carry. So glad you're finally here,* as the couple chatted on.

Mid-sentence I interrupted them, my eyes never leaving that serving counter, "You've never tasted cookies as good as the ones served through that opening right there..." pointing to the serving counter "...Made by a very a special woman..." as my voice whispered into silence.

There, peering around the corner, just above the baseboard where the den meets the kitchen, dangled a white, curlicue cord. PA9-1594 had been ringing – It took me 30 years to get to it – That day I did – and I answered it.

THE FIELDS

The jog back to the church, the final leg I assumed, seemed effortless. Once back in my rental car, a calling of sorts came. Checking my watch, I had just enough time for one more stop; the fields. Behind my high school alma mater is Westbury American Little League, home of the 1966 Little League World Champions. I needed to go by there.

Driving past the old high school, many good memories, some not so good, came to mind. There are the bleachers where I quit the track team. And there's the practice field room where I quit football...and the handball courts where you could buy Quaaludes, Mandrax, weed, just about whatever. Being a rodeo-ing beer drinker, those weren't my drugs of choice, but I did sell a couple of Maalox antacid tablets there for lunch money one morning.

Once past all that I pulled up to the fields. To my surprise, the gates were unlocked and open, as if awaiting my arrival - I drove in. No games going on, just a few pickups parked here and there; Dads mowing grass and grooming the infields, but nothing much else. It was quiet there.

Slow-rolling my rent car down the center lane of the fields, windows down, as the gravel crunched under my tires, I passed the fields one-by-one. There's the concession stand where free snow cones were given in exchange for returned foul balls (Bubble Gum Blue was my favorite). I could still see Mrs. Stockman in there making Frito pies as her cigarette ash teetered a good inch and a half off the Virginia Slim dangling from her lips.

The welded, rebar concession stand windows hadn't changed either. Through them we'd get our "double treats" after a win. Losers got "single treats". Not everyone got a trophy back then.

Ahhhhh...the dugouts...where the lone bag of ice would sweat as it melted up next to the chain link fence in front of the bench. We got one bag of ice per game. No watercoolers or Gatorades. We ate ice. The kids riding the pine at least had the privilege of sucking the melted ice water out of the corner of the bag while the others played the field; was a bummer to come off the field to a dry bag.

There's the field I "parked one" as a 10-year old when I accidentally made the Majors. Wasn't supposed to but tried out "just because"...and got drafted.

And there's the Pee Wee field where Danny Quinlan and I hit back-to-back homers as 9-year olds, against Pearland in a post-championship exhibition game. Still have the ball.

And...there it is...the dugout that called me...the dugout where it ended. I parked the car, sitting there a few minutes, arguing with myself about being there. I eased out and reminiscently walked behind the backstop and leaned against it, reaching up with both hands, my fingers gripping the wire strands of the chain link...and hypnotically looked through the fence out and across the field. It seemed like yesterday.

As if watching the game again, though this time a spectator, time rewound itself; it was late summer '79 and I was at the plate. Making my way behind the first-base dugout, I could see the bench. Entering through the waist-high chain link gate, onto the field and into the dugout, I took a seat and watched the game.

Though only the breeze whistling through the chain link could be heard, with all else silent, suddenly the sounds of gloves popping, "Give it a ride, Jimbo", "You got 'im, Scotty" and "One more, Danny" came alive. I sat, staring into the infield, watching the game that was long ago and, I thought, long gone. "Two down and one to go" is what hit me.

A good little leaguer I was – Starter - Top five in the lineup - All-Star at 12, and again at 15. My final year at Westbury American - Senior Majors - All-stars District Championship against Pearland, I was 15. I'd had a great year, playing left and center, a double handful of stolen bases and batting north of .300. We'd won three straight in the post-season and were ahead late in this game, but playing Pearland would be different this time for me; no back-to-back homers with Danny Quinlan that night - I went 0 for 4, whiffing all four at-bats. I was the "Two" in "Two down"

Until that night there wasn't a pitcher I was afraid of. I mean there were a bunch of guys I'd rather not have faced but no one I was truly afraid of. And this guy wasn't throwing hard or wild... so there was nothing really to fear...except that I just couldn't hit the guy! What's there to fear? Failure...and I knew nothing about that.

A 15 year old, spoiled rotten, hormonally imbalanced, hairball-of-a-mess, I slammed my helmet in the on-deck area and sailed my Louisville Slugger into the dugout fence a little harder with every K. I can't recall ever being more frustrated...with no calming presence to be found.

As if bound and constrained in an emotional straightjacket, I threw myself down on the bench as my coach and team mates moved away from me, without a word. I wouldn't have talked to me either.

An internal inferno, my jaw clinched and a red face filled with tearful frustration, I was inconsolable - Ed Hornsby had seen enough and made his way from the stands to the chain link gate by the dugout.

Completely self-absorbed, I grew madder and more frustrated as my team mates hit the guy one after another "Crack" "Whack" as his curveballs, I couldn't have hit with a tennis racket, ricocheted off their wood bats. I wasn't mad at them - I was mad at him. He withheld from me what I wanted, and a spoiled rotten *anyone*, who is used to getting what they want - and doesn't - is a terror to themselves and everyone around. I couldn't hit him - and I blamed him? That's messed up…

Yanked from the lineup, as any good coach should've done, I was benched as the third out was made on a deep fly ball to center. I'd made the third out the inning before and the second one this time around. I'd ride the pine - but I wasn't about to suck that ice bag.

As the blue and whites took the field I wouldn't look at him. I knew he was over there. Turning my head slightly to my right, as if watching right field warmup I caught a glimpse. There he stood, leaning against that waist-high, chain link gate…watching me. Encouraged, for some strange reason, I looked right at him, and wished I wouldn't have. Now eye-to-eye my face flood flowed even more, in further frustration. As if back in the batter's box, he threw a pitch I'd leaned into and took right in my earhole.

Speechless, he shook his head slowly, side to side, as he watched me spiral down even further. With a look of utter disappointment he walked away - and never mentioned it again. Another K; now 0 for 5.

We won that game but lost the next. I sat the bench, rightfully so, and never played another inning of organized baseball. Having enough raw talent to easily have played high school ball and, with some effort, probably at the next level. But, I was a quitter, a manipulative, someone else's fault quitter.

Although we never had any sort of closure conversation, ultimately Dad accepted what he was dealing with and redirected his fathering toward me as more of a savior, bailing me out of every tough situation I encountered. As he became savior I became savee; we were dysfunctionally perfect for each other.

Now, there I was, at 54, same bench, same gate. Looking slowly to my right...there he stood, yet again, now at 90, watching the same game as I. But this time, as he looked over at me, back to the infield then back to me, his expression was different; still speechless, just different.

We both had something to say. Who'd go first?

Returning my gaze to the infield, something came over me and washed through me.

John, He needs you right now...He needs your forgiveness and wants to make it right...He fathered you all the best he knew how to...He won't be with you much longer and wants to tell you he is sorry, but doesn't know how to...He was never allowed much of an emotional connection with anyone, except me...He loves you more than you will ever know...Love him like I know you want to.

Leaning against that same gate, forearms resting on the top edge, as before, expectantly, hopefully, Dad looked at me...

Overwhelmed with compassion, I couldn't take my eyes off of him...I spoke first...

Dad, thanks for all you've done for us...I've blamed you for too long... You pushed me, then spoiled me and protected me and rescued me... because you love me...and I get that and appreciate that...but, you also handicapped the shit out of me by doing so...My immaturity and rottenness is no one's fault except mine...I know that... as my eyes flooded once again, releasing my pent-up, misdirected anger at him...Honestly, Dad, the life you provided was amazing...but The Box you built sucked...and I haven't had it in me to forgive you...until now.

The old man said in reply,

Goose, I'm so sorry...I tried the best I knew how...I took a lot of pride in my career and what it provided for you, Paul, Cristy and your

Mother...but mostly what it provided me; an identity and purpose. I got my cart and my horse ass-backwards sometimes...Trying too hard to make something of myself I missed some things along the way. Forgive me if you can.

Losing your mother tore my world apart, the world I took great pride in building...I got a lot of skin in this game...Grief is something I've avoided all my life...seen too much for one man to take...The only way I know is to control it or escape it...You and your brother and sister just happened to get in the line of fire of all that sometimes...I'm so, so sorry...

The Box disintegrated in that dugout.

Breathing deeply, emptied at last, I looked out into the infield. All was quiet again. The breeze whispered through the chain link of the dugout as the green canvas tarp behind home plate flapped, popping as it will. I stood to my feet and left the dugout. The game was *finally* over.

THE MASTER

Merle and I had been driving pretty good for a few months, back and forth to work and around town without any major issues. And, with a reliable, drivable car, I jumped the gun a bit and prepared to make Merle the high school hot rod I'd been waiting for – and, ultimately, a wise old gentleman named Jerry would help me do just that.

After years of patiently waiting, I finally had a V8 to work with and all I could think about were headers and dual exhaust. Hank and I discussed the brands I preferred and, sticking to my roots, Hooker and Hedman were my header options.

Settling on Hedmans, I placed the order and waited patiently for their arrival, meanwhile tearing the stock exhaust manifolds away, clearing the right of way for the new headers, soon to be snugged into place...and snugged they were - Damn near impossible to squeeze in. Sometimes "Be still and know that I am God" happens when God stills me. He *stilled* me that night.

Laying underneath Merle long after Kim had hit the racks, trying with all my might to maneuver those headers into their place, I set them aside and laid there...underneath Merle...just thinking...*What am I missing here?...Is there any other way I can maneuver these things in?...*That's when I saw it.

Overcome by the excitement of bringing Merle back to life I'd missed, or better yet overlooked, that she had a lot of oil and sludge built up around the front and rear of her oil plan. *Looks like this has been here a good while...and there's fresh stuff here too,* I couldn't help but notice.

I'm all about transparency and living my insides on my outside, but it doesn't take a brain surgeon, or transmission rebuilder, to know that motor oil needs to stay on the inside. Merle had seal issues, which caused me to wonder what all else might be going on...deeper on her inside.

The longer I lay under there the more convicted I became; a set of Cragar 08/61's doesn't make it a hot rod. There was important work yet to be done, *deep down inside.*

Have to admit I impressed myself with the little bit of patience and self-control that was coming out of me. *Where was that coming from?* I lay a little longer, on our cold, grungy garage floor and thought about it...*the motor had to come out.* Headers would have to wait. Best decision I've made in years.

A hot rod friend from church, Mark, advised me on the generalities of pulling a motor and having the block hot-tanked. He then referred me straight to Jerry, asking me, knowingly, "When Jerry's done, who's gonna rebuild it?" to which I somewhat confidently replied "I am", to which he very confidently asked "With whose help?" to which I wisely replied "Yours".

Mark instilled confidence by telling me "You can do it, no doubt, with my help and the rebuild manual – Take your time and call me when you have questions", concluding our conversation with "Pull it, take it to Jerry and we'll see where we go from there - Ask for Jerry or Cookie and tell 'em I sent ya - and that you're not a salesman...They don't do well with salesmen"; advice well-given and wisely-taken.

Another car guru, also named Mark (felt good to be in the club as my middle name is the same) recommended a good place to rent an engine hoist. Off I went, picking up an inexpensive engine stand along the way.

Merle loved being back on the road, doing her thing, and I loved driving her around town, but we both knew the deeper work needed to be done…and it might take a while. Hanging her keys on the hook, knowing she'd be sidelined for a span, was tough, but an important milestone in her transformation. As those two worn-smooth, brass keys, one square headed the other oblong, dangled on that hook in the kitchen I knew I'd one day grab them back for another go at it…and I could hardly wait.

Reading through my shop manual (Merle's came in two volumes. Ol' Joe's just one) the description for pulling the motor made it seem fairly simple, and it was. There's a lot coming and going to and from the motor but, once cut loose, there's nothing to it.

Hood removed and with Kim's help, we rolled the hoist over and above her heart and soul, connected the pull chains and cranked the hoist to take out the slack…Merle's Rocket 350 shifted a bit. We were loose.

Crank after crank it rose slowly from its mounts…then stopped suddenly, jerking backwards. "Something's still connected" Kim hollered. She has to talk louder in tense situations in order to penetrate my MFHS, Male Focused Hearing Syndrome.

"Not sure what this is or what it does, but this braided wire thing is still hooked up" she yelled.

"Oh, crap. That's a grounding strap. I didn't even see it" I yelled back, unnecessarily, as she suffers *not* from MFHS.

"Hand me something and I'll unscrew it" Kim offered.

"See if this'll work" handing her a ratcheted box end wrench she'd given me for Christmas.

"There…Urrgghhh…Got it" she said, as the motor swung freely, dangling from its chains. Kim's a keeper.

Like cardiac-surgeon pioneers Cooley and DeBakey, Kim and I pulled Merle's heart and placed it on the operating table, preparing it for a full makeover.

Over the next few days, Hank and I took great pride in tearing down the internal components of Merle's motor, a forensic analysis of sorts, though not at all qualified for such an autopsy. Parts and pieces were bagged and plastic-toted until no piece remained attached to another. She was broken down as far as possible, leaving nothing but an empty engine block on its stand, anxiously, or not-so-anxiously awaiting its bath in the hot tank.

Weighing a lot less than when hoisted out of its engine compartment, along with Hank's ability to lift ridiculous amounts of weight, as I unbolted the block from its stand, Hank simply held it, lifted it and set it in the plastic tub in the back of my truck. Good guy to have around.

Arriving at Jerry's, I was in for a rude awakening, from a slumber I needed awakening from.

Walking into the shop, an old warehouse, metal-sided building place, they're busyness was unmistakable; a lot of work going on without a lot of customer interaction, if you know what I mean; just hard-working people working hard. There were engines everywhere and guys running heavy machinery I'd never seen. That doesn't mean much as it was my first time in the belly of an engine shop.

Quite a few of them scurried past me, fetching tools, parts, etc., none saying a thing to me; just making sure I knew I was in their way.

Finally, I stopped one of them long enough to ask "Is Jerry or Cookie available?"

"You a salesman?"

"Hell no!" I replied, as if I hated salesmen too. "I got a block I need hot-tanked!" I yelled over top of the machinery noise.

Greased hand extended, Cookie introduced himself, with a welcoming smile "Let's see whatcha got".

Walking outside, to the bed of my truck, I proudly showed him my bare block, telling him I wanted to have it checked out before I rebuilt it. Having me back up to their single door shop entrance, he made small talk as he waited for one of his guys to bring a roller table out to haul the block inside.

"That's a Rocket 350…Damn good motor" Cookie said, looking into the plastic tub. "They're tough as can be…really heavy-built blocks…I bet it's still good to go…but we'll check it out for you"

Beaming with pride, as if I was dropping a field-dressed buck at the processing plant, I was feeling good about the motor I had and the work I'd done. You know what I'm talking about; you feel good about the buck you shot, until you get to the meat processing place. But, if the meat man tells you it's a good buck, then it's validated as a good buck.

Cookie confirmed I had a good buck…then gutted me gracefully as the guy slid Merle's block onto the roller cart. "Who's gonna rebuild it for you?"

Oh, shit…This is going south… "I am?" I muttered, as if asking a question.

"Ok…" looking at the tailgate of my truck…then right at me…"You gotta piston press to press these pins back in?"

"Nope"

"What rebuild kit you lookin' at?"

"Haven't decided" *Who was I kidding? No one; I hadn't even thought about that yet.*

"We'll hot tank the block for you and give it back to you, no problem…but we can rebuild it for you, for a few extra dollars… and you'll know it's done right…it's what we do…Not saying you can't do it…Just saying we do 'em all the time".

From the looks of their shop, I knew he spoke truth. He continued "Do yourself a favor...Jerry will have some time later this afternoon...Come back by and talk to him about it...then decide...We'll do it however you want...Just talk to him first"

I'd just met the man but, from the look in his eyes, Cookie was trustworthy and was trying to help me. They hate salesmen there, and he wasn't *selling* me; he just wanted me to do it right, and they were the best option to do so.

Leaving there I thought about it all the way back to the office. The lamp unto my path had been lit yet that voice in my head was darkening its glow - *You wussy...Always running to someone else...Show everyone what you're made of...For once in your life, do it yourself...*

Later that afternoon, calling it a day at the office, I drove back out to meet Jerry. His shop was much quieter, as his guys had clocked out around 4:00. Returning through that same doorway I'd entered earlier in the day, I met him at his desk, just behind the service counter. Merle's block still lay on the stainless roller cart.

Alone, except one helper sweeping in the back storage area, sat the man, a lean man, an aged man. Thinly stranded silver hair, slicked back – old school. He sat crooked in his high-back roller office chair, one wheel cockeyed, leaning the chair down and to the left. He seemed in a meditative state, resting from his labors of the day. An aluminum walker, readied to assist, stood by his side, fully-equipped with a tool tray mounted just beneath its well-worn, comfort-wrapped handles. Jerry looked up slowly as I entered the shop and stood quietly at his service counter.

In a voice I had to listen hard to hear...and his every word was worth the effort...,"Whatchu plan on doin' with that motor?" he asked.

"Gonna rebuild it..." I replied, as confidently as I could muster. "...Making the high school hot rod I never had..."

"Ummm hummm..." he interrupted. "Ever done one?"

"No sir...I haven't"

"Not as easy as you might think"

"No doubt...I have the manuals and Mark, the guy who referred me to you..."

Again, he interrupted "You get that motor running yourself the first time?"

"Yes sir, I did" I said proudly, fetching the bone he'd just thrown me.

As he continued "You pull that motor yourself?"

"Yes sir. Me and my wife pulled it..."

"Ummmm hmmmm" he said mid-sentence. "You gonna put it back in there once it's rebuilt?"

"Yes sir" I chose not to say anymore.

"Why you wanna rebuild it so bad? Whatcha after?"

What a great question...How did he know to ask that? I wondered.

"I want the pride and satisfaction of showing myself I could do it"

"Whatchu've done already and what you'll do once it's rebuilt... that's more than 99% of these hot rod junkies out there anyhow!" he said with some passion. "You outta be proud already in what you've done".

Where you been all my life, old man?

"Well...ha ha...you make a great point, Jerry" feeling now more confident calling him something other than "sir".

"For a few dollars more, I can rebuild it for you..." smiling ear to ear, looking me right in the eye "...and you'll know it's right... One mistake on your part and you'd wreck all the good work I've done...Think about it and lemme know."

"I'll do that, Jerry. Thanks. Means more than you know" as he gazed again at the shop floor, seeming tired from the conversation.

"The weekend is coming, so what day is a good day to come back by and let you know?"

"I'm here every day, sunup to sundown...My guys come and go... but I'm always here"

"Sounds good...Give me a day or two and I'll holler back at ya" as I left the shop and drove home.

The next morning I drove to Dad's for a visit, figuring I'd talk it over with him...seek his counsel. He loved hearing about Merle and her progress.

Telling Dad my desire and dilemma, I over-confidently explained that I'd planned to rebuild the motor myself...blah, blah blah (a grown-ass man I was, yet still trying to impress my Dad) ...then I told him about my conversation with Jerry.

"Sounds like a pretty wise old bird" said Dad. He always referred to others as "old", but rarely himself. When delivering Meals on Wheels, Dad would say "I'm out delivering food to the old folks", while he was a good 10 years older than most of his meal recipients.

"You're right about that...Jerry really knows his stuff"

"Maybe you oughtta take his advice"

"I really wanna try and rebuild it myself...I don't know...Maybe it is a better idea to let him do it..." I seesawed back and forth.

"Sometimes ya gotta get out of the way and put it in the hands of the master" he said, looking at me as if waiting for me to come around.

Where's this coming from? I wondered...

"I think I'll call him" as I reached for my phone.

A few days later I made my way back out to Jerry's with the bed of my truck loaded with everything I had torn apart on the motor. He had instructed me to "...just bring it all and I'll send back what all I don't need"

Jerry didn't exactly greet me at the door but waited for me behind the counter as I entered his shop. As his guys hauled my plastic tubs into the shop he looked them over, sifting through the parts, occasionally shaking his head slowly in disapproval as he did so. "You mark any these bearings?"

"No sir"

"No...Of course you didn't...We'll figure it out..."

Pushing the cart to the side, as if casting it into an abyss, he returned behind the counter and continued his interrogation. Funny thing, I didn't seem to mind his off-the-cuff comments and rhetorical, sarcastic questions; I trusted him and knew he really cared about me and my work. Growing up hating that kind of authoritarian dominance, for some reason, I didn't seem to mind it from Jerry.

"What intake you thinking?"

You're asking me? I'm just glad I know what one is..., I thought. "Thinking Edelbrock Performer" I said, as if asking, *Is that the right answer?*

"Ya...I'd go Edelbrock but I'd go with this one right here", scanning the options then pointing to a specific one in his catalog.

"I trust you, Jerry"

"You're going back stock; Right?"

"Yes sir...I just want a daily driver with some punch to it...I'm not looking for bragging rights on Saturday night" He laughed as I said that.

"I'll keep it stock but we'll put a little cam in it to make it fun to drive" he said, grinning.

"Ya...With the motor I'm gonna build you, this one'll work best"

"What carb?" he inquired.

"I'm thinking of matching the intake with an Edelbrock carb... What do you think?"

Shaking his head again slowly in disapproval "Nah...I'm a Holley man. I'd go with a 660"

"You tell me, Jerry"

"While we're at it, I'd put an MSD distributor on it...Like that one right there" he said, pointing again to the catalog.

"When you need it?" he asked.

"Jerry, I've been working on this car for a long time...I'm in no real hurry, plus I have some engine compartment work to do while it's here with you"

"Check back next week" he said.

We shook hands and I left the shop

POBRECITO

Recovery from any addiction requires, what they call, "rigorous honesty" and one of the 12 Steps suggests that we "...admit to God, to ourselves and to another human being the exact nature of our wrongs". God knows me really well, weller than I even know, and being honest with myself hasn't ever been much of a problem, too honest some say, but letting another person in my dark closet was no picnic.

If you've ever stepped in a hot, steaming pile of crap in the yard or out in the pasture you can relate when I say that "deep shit" smells long after the scraping's done. Seems no matter how well you wipe 'em, wash 'em, whatever, after you've stepped in it, a faint-stench lingers on, reminding you what you stepped in... and that there's "deeper shit" still down in there that needs to be dealt with.

That's the way my alcohol recovery had gone; cleaned up pretty good, but I still had some deep shit that I'd stepped in years ago, down in the stitching of my "soul", that was still pretty rank – so I saw my guru, Art.

My guru's one of a kind, a savvy soul who's discovered his authentic self and helps others discover theirs. A rare breed of psycho-spiritual, he calls himself a "Shaman in a Suit". Been referring others to him for more than 20 years now, and began seeing him myself about as long. The Great Spirit that works through him has transformed me in ways I can barely believe and hardly describe, hence why I chose him to complete my Fifth Step.

What happened in my visit with Art spooked me a bit, but, then again, I expected "spook" when he and I would meet. As I laid my deep-shitted boots at his feet, I experienced the divine, the supernatural, in a most beautiful, and badly-needed, way.

Finally letting it out, as the "exact nature of my wrongs" was spoken to another person, here came the associated guilt and shame right along with it. Like a stomach bug that had finally had enough, it cleaned house as I projectile-vomited every ounce of emotion I'd swallowed over the years. He got it all over him...and never flinched.

Simply leaning forward, he patted my knee and smiled ... exactly like Mom had, from the church pew... and recently over our Picasso serving counter...and quietly asked, "John, what would your Mother say to you if she was sitting on that sofa right there?" I broke down and completely lost it – and he let me.

Gathering myself enough to respond, I tearfully, grievingly, looked at that sofa and could see her plain as day, twinning Art's empathetic smile. Paralyzed by her visual embrace, I was unable to speak.

Then, his hand still on my knee, softly he said "You know, John, I think she'd say - 'Pobrecito'". I fell to my knees, sobbing from somewhere deeper in my soul than I knew existed. In a word, I was overwhelmingly embraced by the unconditional love of my Mother, once again, after 30 years of longing for it. I wept and wept.

After a short while, returning to my chair, I looked at him, with a question burning in me. Stiff jaw, in a now defensive tone, I asked "How in the Hell did you know that?"

"I didn't. Do you know what that word means?"

"Yes, I do – Mom called me that all of my childhood – How the Hell did you know that?"

"I didn't." Nodding his head towards the sofa "She did"

RIGHTEOUS BONES

As our conversation continued, the Great Spirit's work continued as well. My shame, guilt and remorse were strangely converted to grace and gratitude for the unconditional love of my Mother and the God she knows.

I got more than my money's worth that day with Art. Not only was I no longer the filthy sinner I'd been taught I was all my life, but a little boy who missed his Mama and acted out his Mama-missin' in some not-so-good ways...and she wasn't nearly as gone as I thought. She was alive and well and as excited as I was to reconnect.

With Merle's motor in Jerry's hands I'd been working on her engine compartment, like an expectant parent preparing the crib for their newborn. After Pobrecito had her way with me that afternoon, later that evening I slipped out into the garage for some therapy of a different kind.

Bluetooth speaker connected, iTunes music tuned in with a good run of Jason Isbell and I was ready to get my hands dirty for a while.

It's knowing that this can't go on forever
Likely one of us will have to spend some days alone
Maybe we'll get forty years together
But one day I'll be gone or one day you'll be gone

Jason Isbell

Turning from my tool chest toward the engine compartment I was stopped dead in my tracks as I was emotionally drawn downward, into the motorless cavern in her chest; her wires, tubing and loosely-bolted brackets dangling purposelessly there; looked like a big stump had been pulled from the ground, leaving root remnants behind.

That hole had me – and Jason's lyrics sucked me down into it like the final half-gallon of water circling the drain - gurgle... gurgle...empty...silent. My salty, grief-ridden tears began to fall as I listened further and looked deeper.

I don't even how to feel anymore, Mom...I miss you...still...so bad... Dad's not doing well...My heart hurts...I still don't know who I am... or even what I'm doing anymore...I'm still trying to be anything and everything everyone else wants me to be...If I could, I would, stay in that moment with you, like earlier today...You left us in the twinkling of our eyes...and left a hole as big as this in our hearts, as I looked down into that empty engine compartment.

The hole then spoke back, *John, Yes, your heart was torn apart... but will return soon...after the work is done...You'll see...Trust me...*

A bar of soap would do that night; I got deep alright...but not deep enough in the grease for Go-Jo. Washing up, I went upstairs. Kim asked if I was ok. I didn't tell her much, just that I'd been thinking about Mom a lot lately, as crawled into bed, laying in her arms as she held me, just held me. Kim's embrace needs no words. Losing her Dad not long before, we held each other...for a good while.

That very night, in the early morning hours, I awakened from a sound sleep, remembering that Dad had asked me to bring him something the next morning as I was heading to Austin for a visit. His high school photograph was one of his favorites of himself and he'd asked if I'd bring it to him the next time I was up his way. His retirement community was having some kind of social where the residents had to guess who was in the old high school photographs. Dad wanted his.

Remembering where I'd been stashing the items Dad unloaded on me each time I visited; I always left with a loaded box or two of stuff he no longer wanted. I split the sheets, slipping out to leave Kim sleeping, and fumbled through the closet in our spare bedroom.

Atop the highest shelf I'd been stacking Dad's stuff, envelopes of pictures and plaques he'd asked me to "find a home for". I knew the picture was up there but had to reach around behind a few items to get to it. Doing so, a blue, hard-backed book tumbled off the top shelf, bouncing on the carpet below landing catty-wampus on the floor, half-opened.

Reaching down to return it to the closet shelf, picking it up, I didn't recognize the book; never seen it before. *Must've been in some of Dad's stuff he had me haul away,* I assumed. Instinctively I smelled it.

Fading royal blue binding, unraveling edges, "Strange Texts but Grand Truths, by Clarence E. Macartney" was gold-leafed on its spine. I cracked it open and took in another snoot-full of its yellow-brown edged pages. "E.S. Hornsby" was handwritten inside. *So it was his...*

Standing in the closet in the wee hours I turned to the table of contents and my eyes were drawn immediately to the bottom of the page, "Chapter VIII, The Influence of the Dead, page 87". Thumbing the page edges, I landed on page 87, which was bookmarked by a crease at the top edge of its page. *Someone had been there, long ago.* I began reading. I can't speak for the other chapters but that chapter alone lived up to the *Strange* in the book's title.

The little blue hardback was a collection of sermonettes written by Clarence Macartney, based on biblical texts rarely preached on. The Influence of the Dead was dead-on and I needed it more than I knew.

Macartney's message was built and based on a brief story in the first testament of the Bible, II Kings 13:21:

And it came to pass, as they were burying a man, that, behold, they spied a band of men; and they cast the man into the sepulcher of Elisha; and when the man was let down, and touched the bones of Elisha, he revived, and stood up on his feet.

His sermonette suggested that the bones of the righteous dead remain able to give new life to us, as we fall down into, are thrown to, crawl to, however we come in contact with them. Our loved ones, the bones of the righteous dead, continue to speak to us...if we have the ears to hear.

...it may have been a day when the stars of faith seemed to have gone out in your heaven. The old divinities were gone; the old beliefs were crumbling; their foundations undermined by doubt or battered by the cruel imagery of life's trials and hardships and sorrow; or their foundations sapped by sin. A gloom was over your soul, and all the birds that sang to you in youth were gone. But in that hour the memory of the just was your salvation. Perhaps you looked upon a portrait which hung on the wall or stood on the desk; and as you looked, the peace and calm of that soul who struggled and overcame through the blood of the lamb was transferred to you. You opened an old Bible, its pages once smoothed by the hands that long had been dust, its verses read by eyes that now beheld the King in his beauty; or you sat again in the church where one whom you had loved and honored worshipped; and faith again spoke its grand music of hope and of triumph, Macartney wrote.

Or, perhaps from the weathered and tattered front seat of a '71 Olds

Cutlass...or through the serving window from the kitchen counter... or the ring of an old phone...

Seeing my dead mother at 5830 Picasso and again on Art's sofa, then hearing her from the engine compartment of my '71 Cutlass, wasn't what roused me from my sleep that night; Dad's high school picture had. Now, in the middle of the night from our spare bedroom's storage closet, I heard her yet again.

There I stood, in the closet but a million miles from anything and everything, as a strange little blue-bound book spoke the words from my dear Mom, the words I needed to hear, and she needed to say. They would define me and my existence, forevermore.

John, he needs you.

Finding Dad's portrait, I placed it in an oversized envelope for safekeeping and set it by my wallet and wristwatch, making sure I'd remember it, as I would be leaving in only a couple of hours to visit Dad. Before enclosing it in the envelope, I double-took the portrait as I swear he was smiling bigger than I'd ever noticed. That little blue book made the trip as well.

Returning to the sack slowly and quietly as possible to avoid waking my sweet Kim, I lay there, as you can imagine, a little freaked and creeped about the day's events. It'd been over thirty years, and I'd longed to see her again, to hear her voice once more; now, in a day or two, she was showing up right regular.

As I considered perhaps more intensive therapy options I drifted back to sleep only to be startled from my slumber by the iPhone alarm. If Old Phone would've ringed I would've postponed my trip to Austin and checked into the state hospital.

HEART OF GOLD

When visiting Dad, if a weekday, I'd leave early enough to miss the San Antonio's rush-hour traffic, but in time to enjoy Austin's version it. This morning was no different. I was on the road at 5:30 A.M.

Knocking on Dad's apartment door at 7:15 I took my usual seat in his desk chair, facing him and his usual seat, the recliner... that he rarely reclined. Usual drill; crossword complete, paper folded, lying beside his chair, directly in his walking path to the bathroom, but he refused to lay it anywhere else.

His Zip-Lock bag of meds was faithfully to his left, on the floor under his TV tray, within arm's reach. Strewn here and there were always a few rogue pills of various shapes and colors along with a handful of wadded tissues...and, there out of sight, therefore out of mind, a crusty, dried piece of cheese from happy hour the late afternoon before...or maybe the day before that.

Handing him his picture, because he was already asking about it as I walked in, he opened the large envelope and slid his high school photo out to show me, as if for the first time. So proud he was of that portrait. He showed it to us often and smiled as he looked at himself; something was in that portrait that he enjoyed revisiting.

Never, ever mentioning who graced me with her presence in the closet a few hours before, I held up the book, asking "You ever seen this? Fell off the top shelf of my closet as I reached for your high school photo", as he reached for the book.

Thumbing through it, then opening the inside cover, as if his signature would confirm it, "Hmmm...I don't recall this book at all..." raising his head to use the reader portions of his progressives "...I don't know..." handing the book back to me "...but then again I don't remember much these days". Untrue but he said that a lot.

When Dad didn't want to talk about something he subtly made it known that he didn't want to talk about that something...and this was one of those times, so I shrugged it off, setting the book by my wallet and keys.

He asked me about the car, always wanting to know how things were going. It was something good for us to talk about, as our conversations were limited when he brought up the current events of Fox News and President Trump. He'd scowl when I'd remind him I didn't watch or listen to the news. He eventually quit bringing it up, and started asking about Merle instead.

"Well...I pulled the motor and tore it down and took it to that engine builder I told you about" as he nodded that he remembered. "Not sure when I'll get it back but I'm not in any real hurry"

"What all's he doing to it?" he asked.

"Stock rebuild, but a performance cam and a high performance intake, carb and distributor" I informed him.

"That's great...that's great...hey, hand me those hearing aid batteries right above...no...there...right there...no...ya...hand those to me...thanks" as he pulled his hearing aids from his ears. Conversation would have to wait. I think sometimes he'd pull that stunt whenever he'd heard enough. Those batteries last more than a couple of days but he interrupted me all the time with that line.

One of my Marks asked me if Jerry had given me an expected completion date. "No…and I didn't really give him one either… You know him better than I do…Should I call or just wait?"

"Picasso the artist never painted to a deadline either…You're working with one of the finest engine artists of our time…However long it takes it'll be worth it", Mark assured me.

As weeks and weeks went by Dad and I continued our visits, always asking me if I'd heard from Jerry. "Not yet, but I'm hoping one day soon" then I'd quote Mark's Picasso line.

"We lived on Picasso Place in Houston…" Dad would say, in response to my comment…

"Ya, Dad, that was a great place; been by there a few times lately. Still looks good. Big trees are gone, but the hood looks good"

"While we're talking about things that take a long time to make…See if that bottle of 14 Hands is open on the counter" *Any way to segue to happy hour…*

Happy Hour at Dad's retirement community was literally from 4:00 to 5:00. Dad's hour of happiness began whenever he wanted.

Once, when asked by a newcomer to the community, "I hear there's a happy hour here in the afternoons. What time does it start?"

Dad humorously replied "4:20…The gathering begins at 4:00 but it gets happy around 4:20". He had a line for every occasion.

As his second glass was poured, he'd usually say "Well, you'd better be hittin' the road…Good to see ya". This was his way of saying *I'm done now and it's time for you to go.*

He and his friend, Bob, would joke with their guests "Good to see you. Come back when you can't stay so long". I think they meant it.

"Hitting the road", I'd beat the heavy traffic and was sailing down I-35 south when I made the call to Picasso. "Hey, Jerry... John Hornsby here. Just checkin' in to see how it's coming along"

"It's ready when you are" he said, as if he'd been waiting on me.

"Great. Tomorrow ok?...Good deal...ok...See you tomorrow"
Click

With my newborn coming home, the nursery needed some finishing touches, so I knocked out the punch-list in her engine compartment late that night. With an un-rimmed spare tire in the bed of my truck, as Jerry had prescribed, I arrived at his shop the next afternoon.

Backing up to that same little doorway, I entered the shop, after quitting time. It was quiet, with just Jerry and two guys there, cleaning up and prepping for the next day's work.

There it was, on an engine stand, clean as a whistle, tight as a drum and ready to roar. "You gonna paint it before you put it back in?"

"Yep...Thinking about going back original Rocket 350 gold..."

"Ya...that'll look good...paint this intake too if you want...I went with a 770 instead of the 660..." as he pointed to the new Holley mounted proudly atop the new intake. It looked like another motor in itself riding up there! It was huge compared to the little 2-barrel I had before.

"School me, Jerry...what changed your mind?"

"It'll run better with this...more like you want...If you end up not liking it we'll swap it out...but I think you'll like it" he said grinning as he would do.

"Take this lifting lug off when you get home...it's ugly"

"Will do...any special oil or break-in procedure you recommend for a rebuilt motor like this"

"Pure 30 weight...none of that other stuff...pure 30 weight...

and once you get it running and set the timing...spin the tires on this thing...that'll seat the rings and set everything like it should be...drive it like you stole it...It's made to run...run it"

Smiling back I replied "I'll do that"

"Now, listen...this motor is designed to run with 12 to 13 volts to the distributor. Your old one had points and condenser and was knocked down to eight and a half or nine...this'n don't'... whatever voltage you got coming from the battery better be going to this distributor" cupping his hand over its cap. "Understand?"

"Yes sir"

"Now, I set the distributor close to where it needs to be...should fire up...might have to set the timing a bit but it's close enough to get ya going".

Wheeling the engine stand to the front door the two guys transferred to the hoist and rolled it outside over the awaiting spare tire. Dropped in and tie-strapped down I signed the check and shook Jerry's hand, thanking him for everything. He'd never fully understand what all he'd really done for me.

Renting the hoist, yet again, Hank and I off-loaded the motor and rested it back on my engine stand, prepping it for its Rocket 350 gold paint job. It came out great, at least in my book it did. My standards are my standards. I refuse to compare myself to others in any fashion. I only compare to and compete against myself; potential self against current self. Therefore, relatively speaking, my engine paint job looked great.

Thank God I'd taken Kim's advice of labeling and bagging every part, nut, bolt and washer during disassembly. I'd have been a lost soul without that.

Like an anxiously awaiting transplant patient Merle longed for her new heart of gold. As the hoist wheeled closer, her heavy motor hovering overhead, swinging slightly from its weight, she practically pulled that thing down into her chest. Halting the hoist, stopping her motor just a few inches shy of their mounts, we bolted the headers in place; much, much easier that way.

With only a slight tilt we snaked the long tube headers backward and downward, straddling either side of the torque converter, settling her motor back into its proper resting place. Snug as a bug in a rug. She'd never looked more beautiful.

After high-fiving and snapping a few photos we began reconnecting the myriad of to's and fro's in and around her heart of gold, referring to Kim's photos more than a few times to remember what connected to what.

Those long tube Hedmans, although a perfect fit, made clearances even tighter around the motor. The work was more tedious than ever before but, as the nights grew longer, and much later, we inched closer and closer to first-fire.

Raustin and Hannah Jo were over one evening and helping me out in the garage. "There Raustin...Agghhh...Think that should do it" as I tightened the electrical lead to the impossible-to-reach starter. "Run get Kim and Hannah and tell 'em 'It's time!'" I said, with a sense of complete satisfaction.

There they stood, cameras up, smiling with eager anticipation. I was nervous about the neighbors, as Merle was now sporting open headers and the time of night was well beyond quiet hour.

"Here goes" as I took my seat in her. The key buzzed as it inserted into the ignition. *Guess we got juice* I gratefully said to myself.

Turning the key, with eager anticipation, watching their faces to enjoy their excitement...Crickets..."Ha...uhhh...Hang on...", turning the key even harder... Crickets... "What the...?" as the crowd offered their consoling advice.

"Could it be the battery?" "How about...?" I stopped listening and wasn't in the mood for new ideas. *I gotta work on that.*

"I don't know" I said in exasperated failure. "It's late…Let's call it a night…"

Raustin was YouTubing but not finding anything. Before I knew it he was in the manual. We found the wiring diagram in the back of the manual; looked like a print out after you're printer has gone haywire. Lines everywhere that seemed to have neither rhyme nor reason.

We carefully traced the lines that we'd rewired, making sure all was according to the diagram. "Hmmm…Ummm hmmm…Yep…Ahhhh….No…It's there…" "I dunno, man…Best I can tell we have it all right…Let's get you guys on the road…It's late…" as we closed her down for the evening.

Of course, I thought about it all night. *Red wire…Green wire…I had power here…Maybe check…*

Hank was chomping at the bit to get over there and they had the chance to come over the next evening for another try.

We retraced all the work Raustin and I had done. Hank'd been thinking about it all night as well. Diving into the manual, we checked every line with an ohm meter, confirming connectivity between components.

"What's this little switch here, Dad?" asked Hank as he pointed to something on the diagram. It was so small it looked like a piece of grease grime stuck on the page. It wouldn't flick off so we looked at it more closely. "Your eyes are better'n mine…What's it say?" I asked Hank.

"Uhhhh…says something like 'Back-up, Neutral Safety Switch'…"

"Lemme see…" I said, as Hank instinctively pulled it up on his smart phone. "Here it is, Dad…It's on the steering column"

Lying backward on the floorboard, crawling up underneath the dash, *Sure enough…there it is…*

"Hand me that volt meter and let's see if we got any power to it...Thanks"

"Nope...Dead" reaching for my tools to remove it. *How the heck had it gone bad just sitting in the garage?* I wondered aloud.

"Dad...old stuff just breaks sometimes...just from being old..."

"Hey! What are you saying?" as I moaned and groaned crawling back out from under the dash.

We called the parts house and, believe it or not, they had the part, but across town at their warehouse. "Hank, ask them if they have a new starter too...Better to be safe..."

"Yep...They do"

"Tell 'em we're on our way"

Back at the house, parts in-hand, we took that impossible-to-reach starter off one last time and bolted on the new one. Hank installed the new switch and we were ready for another turn of the brass key.

Kim was long ago in the bed and no need to awaken her just for another failed attempt. It was straight up midnight.

The neighborhood was sleeping peacefully, roads empty and quiet, with only an occasional cricket chirping in harmony with the sound of night silence.

"Hit the carb with the starter fluid...and let's see if we get any fire" as I eased back into her driver's seat.

I swear I barely turned the key and that motor roared like a caged lion, scaring the "you know what" out of us! Hank laughed and instinctively grabbed his groin, like we men do. Hank hit it again with the ether and as I carefully turned the key she came to life. It sounded like we were in the pits at a NASCAR race. Hank and I were both laughing hysterically and trying to talk to each other but neither could hear the other over the majestic, pipe organ melody her Hedmans played most beautifully.

We let her run, revving her RPMs as Jerry had instructed us, before shutting her down. Kim had awakened, as had most of the neighborhood, and stood on the garage stairs smiling right along with us.

There she was...the high school hot rod I finally had. She had spoken, loudly "The Word of the Lord" to which I responded "Thanks be to God"

As Hank left the driveway, heading for his own home, I pulled the string turning off the overhead garage lights, after one more look at her new heart of gold. As I silently looked there I recalled Mom's words once again...my new heart *was* in place – and running as good as hers'.

TIMING IS EVERYTHING

They say "Timing is everything" and, whoever "they" are, are right. Merle would fire up on command but, under any load, she'd stumble pretty badly. Turned out "they" is Jerry. He'd told me the initial timing was set close-enough to get started but might need some adjustment. As always, he was right; we had some adjusting to do.

The only timing light we had was an antiquated, chrome rig that Dad and I used on his old Jeeps and my '71 Ford truck. I'd hung onto it and kept it in my grandmother's old blue tackle box, just like Dad did. It still worked.

Hank's Father-in-law, Katy's Dad, a good friend, car guy, whatever you wanna call him (We call him "JD"), spent the good part of a Saturday with us trying to get Merle timed.

Much better than I with a timing light he gave it a go and we had Merle running much better. Then, with YouTube's help and a few more adjustments, Merle was daily drivable and getting me to and from work; but I could tell she was still a ways from her best.

Opinions are like you-know-whats, everybody's got one, and they all stink. Asking car guy after car guy, I couldn't get a straight answer out of anyone. Maybe I should've consulted some car *girls*. Telling Dad about it during one of our visits he asked a very simple question "What's Jerry say about it?" *Now that's a great question...and one I hadn't thought about...* I thought to myself.

True be told, Jerry was the last guy I wanted to *have* to call. In Jerry's mind I was in the 1% who did the deeper work; I had no desire to be considered among the commoners, the "junkies" he called them. But, deep-down, I knew Dad was right, so, humbling myself, I made the call.

"Cookie, John Hornsby here…Y'all rebuilt the Olds 350 for me… Ya…How's it going?" I said.

"Good…What's up?" with no time for chit chat.

"Sooo….She's running, just like y'all said she would, but sluggish and not at her best…at all"

"I messed with the timing some and it helped, but what are the numbers y'all recommend for this setup?"

"Hey, Jerry!" he yelled over the loud machinery in their shop. "Olds 350…stock…rebuild we did…Ya…What timing you recommend?" then cupping huis hand over the receiver as I heard muffled conversation "What did he f@!$ up?" etc. From them, I took it as a term of endearment.

"Between thirty two and thirty six at three thousand…" he then replied "…You got a dial back timing light?" he inquired.

"Probably not" not knowing what that is. "Just an old, chrome, regular one".

"See what you can get it to and holler back at us…alright…you too…later" Click.

Honestly, I didn't want to invest in a dial back timing light, as I was a weekend warrior and couldn't justify the expense. I borrowed a high-end timing light from a good friend and, after installing a tachometer, I got pretty close to Jerry's recommendation. Merle ran much, much better but still not like she should.

One Sunday morning, knowing Jerry would be working quietly in his shop without a lot of people hanging around, I called him back. "If you can get it here, let me take a quick look at it" he offered.

"Great... Thanks. See you in a few"

Pulling into the actual bay of the garage, I was motioned to ease on in...then waved to shut it down. Jerry got one of his mechanics to bring an actual dial-back timing light and the surgeon went to work.

He had me rev it to 3,000 RPM and hold it. He made a few turns on the distributor and backed out from under the hood. "You bring those extra parts I gave you?" Thank God I had.

Handing him the little box of parts, he fingered through them and picked two tiny springs of the same color, as he instructed me on their purpose. "Distributor won't advance enough with these springs...These'll do a lot better", handing them to his mechanic to make the swap.

While under the hood the guy asked me if I wanted quicker acceleration off the line or at higher speeds. I told him "Off the line" and he swapped out the accelerator pump spring while he was at it. She ran much, much better going home, and for the next few weeks...

Driving her to work and back, a few times a week, I began noticing more problems; sputtering, backfiring and hesitation. Asking around, again I was getting a multitude of opinions, none of which felt right. Without further hesitation, I called Jerry again.

"Hmmm...Maybe I put too much carb on that thing after all... Bring it back to me and leave it with me and I'll take a look...If it's too much I'll swap it for the 660"

I dropped Merle back at Jerry's and felt good about her being with a man of his word, like Jerry. He was a humble gentleman, acknowledging that he might have overestimated the carb for Merle.

It wasn't 48 hours later and I got the call. "Hey...found your problem"

"Great...knew you would..." I said overconfidently.

He interrupted "The problem is the guy who put this all together doesn't know what the Hell he's doing!"

Whoever exalts himself will be humbled, and whoever humbles himself will be exalted.

Jerry is truly a humble man, but I was the one needing a humbling...and boy, did I get one. Wished I would've humbled myself instead.

"Ha...Uhhh...You know I'm the one who put it all back together" I said ashamedly.

Calmly he said "I know...I know...Just messing with you...The voltage to your distributor..."

Foolishly, this time, I interrupted Jerry, "...Should be twelve to thirteen volts but it reads eight and a half..."

"So you knew enough to know that...Why didn't you do what I told you to do?"

No need to answer, but I have a bad habit of answering rhetorical questions "It was running good enough for a while..."

"Good enough aint good enough!...I built this motor to run a certain way and if you'd've done what I told you it'd run that way and you wouldn't be back in here...The fuel/air mixture on this set up needs the twelve to thirteen like I told ya...Your voltage aint burning my mix...Make sense?...That's why it's backfiring and running like shit...It's fixed now...and ready when you are"

"Can't thank you enough, Jerry", I said.

"No problem...Call me anytime" he kindly replied.

Kim dropped me back at Jerry's and could barely keep up with me on the drive home. Merle was running like a bat outta Hell... and so was I.

Spiritually back in touch with Mom and emotionally freed from my guilt and shame, my voltage finally caught up with her fuel/air mix. In life, just like in hot rod motors, timing *is* everything and good *aint* good enough.

14 HANDS

D ad was then 91 years young, still quick-witted and sharp as a tack but, as his physical strength and stamina declined, his will to go on did as well. We'd relocated him back to Austin, from Dallas, a year and a half before, after his second wife had passed, hearing him tell us "…it's home for me…it's where I met your mother…where I went to school… your mother's buried there…". It didn't take long to realize why he wanted to go home…he was ready to go "home", and when Dad's ready to go somewhere, he's ready to go.

With Dad's health issues becoming a more regular thing, conversations between Dad, Paul, Cristy and me began as we considered options for him going forward. He was gaining frequent flyer miles at the local emergency rooms, with overnight stays and follow-up visits out the yin-yang. He was tired of it all and looked to us for options.

Dad, like most men of his generation, sized people up quickly, according to what they brought to the table. He saw everyone as subject matter experts of something. During this sacred time in Dad's life he anointed each of us for something, explicit scopes of responsibility as well as "…other duties as assigned…", having individual conversations with each of us, informing us of our roles. Those conversations were special and meaningful to each of us, just as he intended them to be.

Paul was executor of his estate, handling all financial and legal matters; perfect choice. Cristy was daily caregiver and companion, doing anything and everything he needed around the house, prescriptions, etc. She sacrificed a lot to relocate to the area and care for Dad. She was also a perfect choice.

Kim was designated his cup bearer, a.k.a. wine partner. Having lost her Dad not too long before, Dad knew she needed some grace, and for him to drink *socially* he needed someone there for it to be "social". Poor Kim played her role well. I can't say "perfect choice" as that wouldn't make Kim look good. I was her designated driver home after every visit.

Yours truly, he anointed as his pastor...no sweeter words had I ever heard from him. At 54, still feeling like I needed his approval, that I impressed him somehow, that he thought I was worth a shit...and he confirmed all of that in one conversation.

"John, I'm gonna need you to get through this...You know, pastor me a little, like you know how to do" he said solemnly, eye-to-eye with me. I knew he meant it.

Collaborating behind his back, we made sure each of us knew the roles and responsibilities he'd laid out, coordinating his additional needs with our schedules. I couldn't have dreamed of a better team to work with.

Late one night in the hospital, he woke me from my not-so-deep roll-a-way bed sleep to inform me what he'd been thinking about...and he was always thinking about something. He was ready to go, not checking *out* of the hospital, but checking *in* at the Pearly Gates.

"Well, Dad, let me take a leak real quick and we'll talk about it..." I mean, being awakened by your elderly Dad with "I'm ready to go..." requires you to take minute and gather your thoughts. Mine were gathered standing straddle-legged over his hospital room toilet, dodging that little plastic cupped-catch-all in all hospital toilets - around 3:00 A.M.

He pressed on with the kind of talk we'd been hearing from him lately, how he wasn't "...able to do this and that" and wasn't "...feeling well and was tired of the hospital scene...This no way to live".

I humorously replied "Well, Dad, I can't exactly put a pillow over your face when the nurse turns her back..."

"I know...I know" as he laughed. "Let's look at other options... Ok?"

"You bet, Dad...We'll do that" as I slipped the short-sheeted roll-a-way covers back up over me as best I could, thinking to myself *Mom, I now know what you meant...He does need us...and now I know why...*

First thing the next morning I called his in-home health provider to discover they provided palliative and hospice care as part of the program. They were well-aware of Dad's medical history and current situation. The next step was evident and they were more than willing to help with this conversation. It went something like this.

The palliative care coordinator scheduled a visit late the next afternoon. We three kids were present and accounted for. The coordinator arrived right on time, a good start with Dad, and did a great job all the way through. We can't thank her enough.

She introduced herself and humorously lightened the mood as she kicked-off the meeting about Dad "kicking off". Dad "sized her up" before she said "Hello". He liked her, and that's what mattered most to us at the time.

Remember, in Dad's Box, if you looked good you had a chance of being listened to. Throughout his ordeal, he'd refer to her as "She's the pretty one". Whatever it took; we didn't care. She made an immediate connection with Dad. Check.

Her voice softened as she professionally and compassionately described the experience of palliative care and the patient experience with conditions like Dad's. As she talked, he'd look at me then look back to her, back at me, back at her. As she was beginning to retrace her steps, Dad realized it and begin to look my way with an expression of *Is this something we need to consider?*

After his second look, I spoke up, looking at her as if *Let me translate this for him.*

"Dad, your boiler feed pump isn't able to keep up with the pressure and temperature of your unit and it's causing performance issues, big time. They're working hard to relieve the pressure but your unit can't keep this up long-term" Being a mechanical engineer, he grinned and nodded approvingly

"And replacing the boiler feed pump isn't an option; is it?" he asked rhetorically.

"That's correct, Dad" I compassionately assured him.

He looked back at her and said "The life-cycle of a coal-fired power plant is 40-45 years and at 91 I've outlived two of those. With what I've got going on here it looks like we need to ride this horse into the sunset...Where do I sign?"

Looking over at me with a look of *Did that just happen?* I answered with a speechless nod as she slowly handed the form and pen to Dad for his John Henry.

Handing it back to her "So, how long is this gonna take?" It's always been much more about the destination than the journey with Dad. In his business mind, he had just negotiated a deal, signed the contract and wanted to know when his project would get underway and when it would be commercially complete. Dad was Point A to Point B with no time for anything inbetween. Dad didn't *not* want to be here, he simply *preferred* to be elsewhere; par for his course.

She explained that a nurse would be coming by his apartment, once he was discharged, to explain the process further. She then stood, shook Dad's hand with a look of *I've never met a palliative/*

hospice patient quite like you, but I like it and left.

"Well, I think that went pretty good…and I feel good about the plan…She's a good-lookin' gal isn't she?"

Returning home to his apartment the next day, the nurse came by to introduce herself. She was good but had no idea what she was getting into with Dad. Initially speaking to him in very slow, louder than normal, hospice baby-talk, often talking to us, assuming he wasn't able to understand, Dad interrupted her with "Can someone tell her I'm sitting right here and hear everything she's saying" in a sarcastic, mimicking, very slow, louder-than-normal patient reply.

We quickly but gently informed her that "Dad's fully capable of having these conversations – He did the New York Times Crossword with an ink pen this morning before the paper delivery guy got back to his van and wrapped up a call with his financial broker as you arrived. He's good for these conversations"; we should've asked if *she* was.

She held up the infamous brown paper sack of hospice medications, telling him they would be in his refrigerator when he became uncomfortable. "Define uncomfortable" again negotiating the contract terms.

Still slower and louder than necessary, she said "When your condition causes pain or you become anxious…" He interrupted "When I become *uncomfortable*…" sarcastically using finger quotes "…and I begin these medications, can I still enjoy some good red wine …and a scotch?"

Looking over at us like *What's happening here?* she smiled and said "Ed, you're on hospice now. You can do whatever you want" with a big, happy, hospice smile. If shit-eating grin had a picture in the dictionary, Dad's would be there.

"You have no idea what you just told him" I interjected. "Dad, as your pastor, I want you to know that The Good News of the gospel just got better for you. Proverbs 31:6 tells us 'Give strong drink unto him that is ready to perish, and wine unto those that be of heavy hearts'. Even God says it's ok for you to partake"

"That's the best sermon I've ever heard...and I think I'll take you up on that!" as he raised his hand, pointing to the ceiling as if *Amening* a good sermon.

Having a good laugh the nurse left and Dad looked my way saying "I'm feeling a little broken-hearted" again with the finger quotes, as he motioned for me to open his favorite cabernet for his afternoon therapy. As I uncorked his wine, he said "She's a pretty good-lookin' gal too", smiling as he returned to his afternoon news television.

We walked alongside Dad through the next three months, watching him grow evermore impatient as time moved to the right. He was ready to go and minced no words in telling everyone that. In Dad's mind it shouldn't take nine months to have a baby, a half-hour to drive through the Holiday Christmas Light Wonderland (he did in eight minutes, tailgating the guy in front of us with his hand on the horn) and immediately after signing hospice paperwork he thought he should've been next in line at the Pearly Gates.

I'd make my early-morning trips a day or two a week, alternating days with Paul and Cristy, heading south around lunch, getting in half-days at the office. Never a morning drinker, Kim made the afternoon trips with me. Merle would drive me when I went solo and the weather cooperated. We'd stop by the cemetery to see Mom on our way out of town.

Our coffee talks, he drank Ensure, were mostly consumed with a cursory review of his prescription list and a third or fourth time to remind him that he no longer needed his "preventive" meds, as we were no longer trying to "prevent" anything. I'd happily remind him a million times more, if I had the privilege.

Once the prescriptions were agreed to, we'd work on getting his sound back on his television, usually muted accidentally by a remote control button he'd accidentally pressed. One morning he watched the news in Spanish because he had somehow changed the language preferences on his remote. He knew only a few words in Spanish, all nouns, but spoke them confidently as if making sentences. They made no sense at all but it was funny as Hell.

After his stars were aligned, once again, he and I found ourselves in deep conversation. Not long conversations, mind you, but deeper than he and I had ever gone.

Somewhat jokingly, half-cockily but with newfound confidence, I said "Now Dad, since you've anointed me as your pastor through this, our conversations will be a bit different than before...When Reverend John shows up he will ask deeper questions and talk about deeper things than when Johnboy who's losing his Dad shows up...That ok with you?" making sure he and I were aligned per our contract and scope document, as he would say.

Looking at me with a smirk, but a proud smirk, amused by my confidence, he replied "Well now, *Reverend John,* you're welcome to go in my back bedroom but you're NOT going in my basement" as he grinned. "Agreed" is all I could muster in return.

Pastoring my dying father was a first for me; you only get one shot at it and this was mine. I'd make the best use of my time with him, by no means pushing his limits. Johnboy had pushed his limits a few times as a kid, never finding it worthwhile. Pastoring E.S. Hornsby would be done his way...but Reverend John was a far cry from Johnboy. I'd push his limits as they needed to be pushed.

Awaking from an afternoon fog of a nap with "Hey...there's a story somewhere in the Bible that talks about who you'll be married to in Heaven...Remember that one? Ask that smart phone of yours about it", Dad instructed.

Laughing, I asked, as I looked it up, "What's on your mind?"

"Just read it"

"Well, Dad, that's a story about some religious nuts trying to trick Jesus by asking about resurrection...not exactly about marriage..."

"Ahhh...I see", said he.

"But Jesus does let them know that, unless you follow the Latter Day Saints tradition, there is no marriage in Heaven, but we're like the angels...children of God...brothers and sisters, kinda..."

"OK...Good...So I shouldn't be concerned if they're both there?" referring to Mom and his second wife.

"You crack me up, Dad...It's way late to be concerned about them being there or not, but according to our faith tradition there's no worry about which one you'll be married to...You good with that?"

"Yeah...I'm good with that" as he went back to opening his mail.

"How's your car running?"

"Like a bat outta Hell"

"Atta boy...That's fun...Isn't it?" He'd then retell stories about old Jeeps he rebuilt, later remembering that I rebuilt them with him.

"Sure is, Dad. Sure is"

After "ensuring" he was stocked up on Ensure and 14 Hands cabernet I kissed his forehead, bid him goodbye and headed to the cemetery. I'd been there only occasionally over the past 30 years but, now, every chance I had, I'd stop by there as I left town.

Austin Memorial, once a sad place for me, was now sacred and somewhere I just couldn't seem to stay away from. I felt a presence there, a loving embrace there, her there. Their double headstone had more of my attention now as his Pearly Gates were now in range.

As I'd look at Dad's side of the headstone, with his name, birth date and dash etched into the grey granite, I'd wonder what the second date would be. As if standing right beside me, embracing my left arm, I'd hear - *You're doing well, Reverend John.* Her validation meant even more.

> *Spirits are using me, larger voices callin'*
>
> *What Heaven brought you and me cannot be forgotten*
>
> *Crosby, Stills and Nash*

Knowing where this was headed, as Dad would often remind us "None of us get outta here alive", I tried my best to enjoy every moment we had together, and did, especially his final few months.

Leaving Austin Memorial Cemetery, hitting the gas on I-35 south, in a '71 Olds Cutlass named Merle, I continued to fall apart, all the while coming together. I was dying right along with them, yet being born again all the while.

IT'S TIME

Cold brown bottle, do your magic one more time

Walt Jr.

Visiting one of our jobsites south of Houston, I was on an overnight run, away from home, when I got the call. Dad's hospice nurse was on the line to inform me "Your father's *really* becoming uncomfortable..." As she explained his situation, we both knew it was for real this time.

During some of our deeper conversations I'd asked Dad "Are you really ready to go?...You know me...I'm not evangelizing you or any of that...I really just need to know if you're *really* ready..."

Confidently and calmly "I am, John..." he began "...I know *where* I'm going...I know *why* I'm going and I know *who* awaits me there" he said with a longing smile. "...I don't think it's like they taught us in Sunday School but I think it will be wonderful and I'm looking forward to it".

Had to be one of the calmest and most confident responses to that question I'd ever heard, and I've held the hands of many a transitioning soul.

The nurse loved Dad and we are forever-grateful for her. Now and then the *right* people show up at just the *right* time...Coincidence?

Agreeing that his discomfort was an issue she explained how things would look going forward.

My guru and I were meeting regularly throughout this, as were I and a handful of faithful friends in "the business". I learned that, even though I'd done this type of pastoring hundreds of times, when it's your own flesh and blood it's different, therefore I sought outside counsel. I was blessed with a handful of the best. Darwin, Jane, Deana, Charlie, Paula and Alan; for you, we are forever grateful.

Perhaps you've experienced as well, God's sense of timing is more precise than even Jerry's. My guru had recently taught me something that I'll ever-remember; the difference between a preacher, pastor and...medicine man. Sounds like the lead-in to a good joke, but it's no joke.

"John, a preacher gives a good word to the congregation, a pastor makes people feel better when they're hurting...and a medicine man helps 'em get where they're trying to go" Like a good piece of jerky packed in my saddlebag, that morsel would feed my soul when I needed it, just a little further down the trail. I was there now and reached for it.

The nurse explained how the medications would be administered; we would be doing the administering. She would provide the first dose and we would take it from there, per her prescribed regimen and dosage. Dad was a classy drinker, never a brown bagger, but the infamous brown bag was finally hitting the scene.

While still pulled to the side of the road, as we concluded our phone call, I reminded the nurse who she was dealing with and of his impressively-high tolerance for mind-altering substances. She laughed and said "Thanks...Good to know" and hung up.

As I returned onto the highway, though the sun was rising behind me, it was setting in Austin. We had now mounted his horse and were riding west, into the sunset, just as he'd wanted for a long, long time.

Cristy was in route and had that Wednesday covered. I shuffled the calendar to be with him Thursday and Paul would take Friday. We'd take it day by day from there.

Arriving early on Thursday, Cristy briefed me on the medication drill. Nothing complicated about it, but I wanted to make sure I didn't screw it up somehow. Preaching and pastoring I was cool with, as I'd been doing that for years, but this medicine man thing was new…and would end up impacting me in ways I couldn't have imagined.

Cristy hit the road, as Dad had fired a warning shot at her "You'd better get on the road I guess…You've done a great job but you have other things to tend to…", he'd say when he was ready for us to be somewhere other than with him.

"So, what time do I need my next dose?" he asked me. "Dad, it's only been a half-hour…It's gonna be a little while…I'll let you know…Probably around noon or so"

"Ok…So, whatchu been up to at work these days?" he asked. We then chit-chatted for a while, watching the news and checking his email.

I'd ask "How does that stuff make you feel?" to which he'd reply "I feel good…Can't really feel much of anything…Just makes me a little sleepy but not bad"

"Are you hurting anywhere?" I asked. "Nope, not a bit", he said, as if feeling *really* good.

"Good. Your nurse really knows her stuff" I said back to him.

"Ummm hmmm, but I'll tell you the best one is the gal who comes every Tuesday and Thursday morning for my bath! She's the best doctor I have!" as his eyes lit up and he smiled, continuing on with way more detailed information than either John-boy or Reverend John needed to hear.

I figured *Hey…He's 91 and on his way to the sweet bye and bye…Why not let him enjoy, not only shower time, but telling me all about it.*

We ordered lunch; always BBQ, tacos or Chinese. Dad did really well taking good care of himself along the way but when the brown bag came out of the fridge, he began enjoying what would be his "last suppers", so to speak. After all, he'd been licensed to "…do whatever you want…" by his nurse.

After lunch we relaxed in the easy chairs and "Lets' see what Trump's up to" watched the afternoon news, knowing full-well I couldn't have cared any less about what Trump was up to…So I checked emails of my own, making sure my job was taken care of, while I was there caring for him.

As you do with dying people, I looked over at him a lot. As I did, I caught him napping, a rarity for him. *Hmmm…that's weird… must be the meds,* I thought to myself.

Although knock, knock, knocking on Heaven's door, Dad wasn't behind the Gates just yet, as I watched his chest inhale and exhale slowly. I smiled to myself, pleased that he was comfortable.

As I hit "Send" to an office email reply he began speaking. Looking at him I was struck by what I saw…and heard.

His eyes remained closed, head tilted to the side and mouth half-open as he muttered "Now I look in a glass darkly, but then face to face. Now I know in part but then I will know even as I am fully known" then silence…eyes still closed and mouth still open slightly.

Amazed and somewhat perplexed I realized that he was quoting, verbatim, a familiar passage of scripture that I knew but would have to look-up. As I began my smartphone research, he awoke for a moment. Groggily, he looked at me, his eyes looked like he'd been down for a long winter's nap, or entertaining customers all night, and sleepily asked "What does that mean?" as if he'd just heard it like I had.

"Well, you just quoted 1 Corinthians 13:12 in perfect King James fashion..." as I laughed to myself in bewildered astonishment. "...This is the Apostle Paul's first letter to the Corinthian church..." I sounded so stupid; as if Dad had turned the channel to a Netflix documentary of "Reverends Gone Wild".

Dad cared nothing for my theological dissertation as his loud mouth-breathing stole my attention. While foolishly trying to explain the inexplicable, I looked back over at him, he was fast asleep again.

That was really weird...What just happened?...Did he really just say what I thought I heard him say?

As I watched him rest, there in his easy chair, I concluded he wasn't asking for his own sake...He was asking for mine. He was literally beginning his journey home, transitioning from this life to the next, and, as he did, he was seeing much more clearly, not as in a *glass darkly*. He was beginning to see *face-to-face*...He was telling me to keep looking into that dark glass...that it was worth it.

He awoke a half-hour later with "Hey, hey..." as if he was embarrassed he'd fallen asleep. Don't know why old people, old men in particular, are ashamed of napping. *"A sign of laziness, John..."*

He had no recollection of that occurrence. I never asked about it and he never brought it up. I looked no further for the passage I'd use at his graveside service.

The night aide we had hired to stay with Dad through the nights had just arrived and we got her settled in with the medication drill and his bedtime routine. It was nearing 7:00 and he was firing his warnings that it was bedtime.

Shakily and unsteady, he began to stand, proving he could still do it on his own. He rose from his throne and reached his left arm in request of a helping hand. The drugs were doing their thing; he was painless, but his mobility took a back seat to his pain management. They told us this would be the case, but he was determined to keep going until absolutely incapable.

Nightshirt on, teeth out, he was in his bed and ready for his rest. He looked up at me and asked the aide to give us a minute. As she politely gave us our space he quietly and emotionally spoke "This is what I'm talking about, John...I can't do the things I used to do...I have no strength left...This is no way to live...Y'all need to move on with your lives...You don't need to be doing all this..."

"Dad, we love you and enjoy taking care of you...it's a privilege...an honor...You know how many dirty diapers you changed for us?"

A whisper chuckle "John...I never changed any of your dirty diapers...Ha..."

"Dad, do you know the only one of the ten commandments that ends with a promise?"

"No..."

"Honor your father and mother...that it may go well with you and you'll live a long and prosperous life...or something along those lines"

"Then y'all oughtta live forever then...Appreciate it so much"

"Dad, we love caring for you. It brings us joy. It's a privilege"

"Well...I'm glad I could bring y'all so much joy...but, I'm ready to go"

"Ha...We know, Dad...We know. You're on your way. Sleep well. Love you"

"Love you too...Tell the gal she can come back in if she needs to...She's a good gal..."

Leaving that night for San Antonio, having to work the next day, I knew those would be our last words to each other.

Too late for Austin Memorial, Merle drove me due south for San Antonio. I hit the gas hard that night. Windows down, the night air is what I needed, as I had a lot on my heart. We'd just laid Ken, my father-in-law, to rest not long before, as well as Dad's wife that same year. I was reaching my emotional capacity limits on the drive home; Reverend John was off-duty; Johnboy now had the wheel, and he was a pissed-off, unresolved grief-stricken, little boy.

Just north of San Marcos, minding my own business in the center lane of Interstate 35, an old P.O.S. Jetta passed me on my right, cutting close in front of me and gave me the bird. Poor choice - Wrong night, wrong car, wrong dead Mother, wrong dying Dad to flip off...

Merle was already doing over 70, as she did *not* do well in the slow lane, but he passed me like I'd been in his way. My flesh over-rode my spirit and I stomped the gas. Merle ran him down effortlessly. It was a poor choice on my part as well...but felt right at the time.

As Merle pulled alongside him he looked over, as if in shock that we could catch him. For the record, Jerry had built a helluva motor and Merle had more than a few horses left in her stable (her frontend might have shaken loose but we had more than enough pedal left).

Anticipating a returned gesture I'm sure, there would be no finger for the pimple-faced, adolescent punk in the Jetta. With Reverend John stuffed in the trunk and Johnboy at the wheel, Merle was actually driving the show, Merle Cloteen that is. Through her eyes, I saw the punk as a hurting little boy who probably felt a lot like I had. I didn't know his story, but could imagine it.

Running near 80, as he expectantly looked back at me, I gave him a compassionate, downward-pointed smile, pobrecito-like...as he backed off and Merle left him in her rearview.

I'd return to Dad's on Saturday, hopefully before the sun had set.

Friday was much the same as Thursday, from what I hear; increasing doses of morphine and anti-anxiety meds, yet Dad had awakened at normal time, showered (assisted by the best doc he had), dressed (always a sharp dresser), perched in his easy chair, read the paper and did the crossword puzzle.

As the dosages increased throughout the day, we assumed he'd be out of it...then we got the call.

My mobile phone rang maybe around 5:30 or so that afternoon. It was from Hannah Jo. If something had happened to Dad, I assumed the call would come from Cristy or Paul, or the hospice nurse, but it was from our sweet JoJo.

"Dad?"

"Hey kiddo..." I said somberly, ready to console her. "...Did y'all make it there ok?...How's he...?...Is he...?"

"Dad! Big Ed's the life of the party! Uncle Paul is here and Cristy, me and Raustin...and...Oh, my God..." as she laughed hysterically. Happy Hour took on a whole new meaning when Big Ed was at the helm.

"Dad, he's telling jokes and has everyone rolling...What's that Big Ed?...Of course...Sorry, Dad. He wants me to pour him another glass of 14 Hands...Anyways, just wanted y'all to know... Love ya"

Kim and I had to laugh. Dad was going out just as he had wanted, surrounded by loved ones, being himself and spouting off one-liners and jokes like only he could do...all the while enjoying his favorite cabernet.

Hannah called us as they left his apartment, letting us know that they got him safely to bed. One last Famous Grouse scotch, comfortably now in bed and "retired", as he would say, for the last time.

Saturday came and I went back to spend the day. Merle and I stopped by Austin Memorial on the way into town. The dash and date were drawing closer together.

My cemetery visit that day was different, more logical, functional and rational. It was now much more congested, as "residents" had moved into the neighborhood over the past 31 years. I'd had a dream shortly after Mom's passing that I was down in the grave with her. She was showing me around, as if inside her new condo, "Yeah, it's got plenty of room…and the *guy next door* hasn't moved in yet so I have all that space as well…" as she hosted me, pointing out the features of her new living space. It looked like an industrial-styled, downtown flat apartment. She was so proud and excited about her new place, and that gave me some much-needed peace back then.

Now, there I stood, looking over the empty lot that would soon be occupied by "the guy next door". I knew she'd be thrilled at his arrival, as he would as well. There'd be a "Welcome Home" party like only she could plan. The last party she had planned was also in Dad's honor; she departed at that one. This one she was planning as well, a celebration that would never end…ever.

During one of Reverend John's visits with Dad, a week or so before, he said "Let's talk through the service" as he leaned back in his chair, legs crossed, elbows on either armrest with hands touching together, each finger with its respective finger on the opposite hand, like a spider doing push-ups on a mirror. This posture meant "negotiation and planning". Seen it all my life and knew the language and frame of mind we'd be working from.

"Look…I don't want one of those services where someone's up there lying about me and everyone's (mimicking cry face) tuning up…Mercy (as if disgusted)…*Geez, no wonder he didn't come to many of my sermons; I cry at all of them*…I think a nice, casual visitation (in his socially appropriate voice) would be good…"

"Ya, that sounds more like you", I assured him.

"See if Weed-Corley can have a nice room set-up where people can visit and socialize"

Weed-Corley was Dad's go-to for funerals in the Austin area. He told Paul, as part of the business end of all this, "Listen, when the time comes, call Weed-Corley and ask to speak to Thurlow. He and Dad are good friends"

Cristy and I were there with Paul when this conversation took place. We laughed in front of him, gently reminding him that, if he did the math, Thurlow, if still alive, would be about 129 years old...but we'd be glad to ask for him when we made the call. Dad returned our laugh...and sipped his cab.

Laughing, he said, "And, if you leave that casket lid open, I'll reach up and pull it down tight. Your Mother and I didn't believe in open casket services". Dad always dropped her name when he wanted no backtalk.

"All sounds good to me" as I made notes from our conversation.

"The next morning I think a small, private, graveside service would be nice...for the family...or whoever might show up... and it should last no longer than fifteen minutes...and you do a brief message...say a few words...You know, a wise man once told me 'the key to a meaningful message is an engaging introduction that really pulls the audience in and a powerful closing that really drives it home...and get those two things as close together as possible!'" as he laughed and looked directly at me as if saying *You understanding that I want it brief?*

Nodding in agreement "Yep...Got it...Be prepared, be brief and be done!" I recited back to him as he had quoted that often as well. He smiled and nodded in utter satisfaction.

"I'll give you a little warning...Others might want to get up and speak...you know preach a little...and you don't let 'em...Your Mother and I didn't ever like that" Here we go again with the name dropping.

"No problem...Every funeral service needs a bouncer....Got it covered" I confirmed.

As I stood...alone...at the cemetery, imagining the scene, along with Dad's contract specifications, running through my head, I thought to myself *Who would show? Where would everyone stand? Should we plan for a dozen?...Fifty? The funeral-appropriate green canopy would seat maybe twenty or so...Who cares?...There's plenty of room...for whoever might show...*

As I arrived at his apartment, meeting Cristy there, as she had slept there beside him the night before, I saw Dad, resting in his bed, way after daylight, for the first time in...ever. His morning paper and crossword lay unopened beside his chair.

He was breathing smoothly and deeply, waking somewhat now and then, only to see who was there. He'd smile in a stoned, happy way and drift back to a peaceful rest.

The doses were increasing as time drew near and I administered them on that Saturday, feeling much more the medicine man than pastor.

He'd wake now and then and motion for his "duck" as he called it (the plastic pee bottle patients use when unable to stand and deliver), rolling his weary eyes back and forth, trying his best to hold them open, as we'd help him *water his duck.*

Those bedside moments with him are sacred, not that I helped him urinate, but that he let me. Dad was the consummate provider for us and considered it a mortal sin to ask for help, or need to. Now, in his dying days, he reached out and allowed us to help him. Every time I take a leak I look down and think of him...and I hear him whisper *Thanks.*

Dad had begun "the rattle" as his breathing became more taxing, painless but cluttered. His other vitals remained stable so, with his history of super-health, I estimated he might live on another couple of days like that, maybe. I kissed his forehead and hugged Cristy before heading south to San Antonio, stopping by Austin Memorial one last time.

A hot July late afternoon, the grass was dry and crispy under my Chuck Taylors. As I walked slowly to their graves I noticed that the somewhat-real looking flowers we had placed there a while back had faded greatly and were in need of freshening up. As if preparing the scene for what would take place there just a few days from then, I pulled the weather-beaten, brittle flower arrangement from the green Styrofoam stuff inside the clay pot, giving it a good yank in the process.

Holding the faded flowers downward, I said to Mom *I know you've both been waiting a long time for this…It won't be long before he joins you. The "guy next door" is moving in shortly.*

I felt an elated peace as an unseasonal breeze washed over me. A sweat-soaked shirt will feel that way with just about any breeze that time of year, but this one felt special.

Walking up the way, to pay respects to my cousin, aunt and grandparents, warning them that Unkie, Eddie and Son was on his way. Before I got to their plots, my left hand, the one holding the faded fake flowers lit up like a red-hot needle was going through the cuticle of my thumb. A stinging scorpion, as Dad used to call 'em, nailed me right in the thin skin of my left thumb's cuticle.

I instinctively screamed "Son-of-a-bitch!" at the top of my lungs and kicked that bouquet as far as I could kick it, running after it and stomping it into the ground before punting it again toward the forest green- painted trash barrel.

Looking over to my left I saw an elderly couple walking to their car, having visited one of their loved ones. The man had his arms around his sweet wife, helping her to their car. She compassionately looked at me, downward smile (it kept happening) and soft eyes as if saying *You poor boy…You're still not over it…*

Damn right I wasn't over it yet. My thumb burned all the way back to San Antonio, even with ice from my fountain drink Mountain Dew pressed on it. Never swelled and felt nothing a couple of hours later, but hurt like the dickens when it hit me. Some things are like that.

Kim had finished her work and was ready when I hit the house. We went to Saturday evening worship together. Can't recall the sermon; didn't matter. We felt the Spirit of God on us and we needed that more than ever about then. We approached the altar and prayed together for Dad to be taken home that night. We knew he would, though it felt good to pray.

> *...for we know not what we should pray for as we ought: but the Spirit itself maketh intercession for us...*
>
> *Romans 8:26*

As we returned to our seats I wrote on the bulletin "Up for a road trip?" Kim smiled and nodded *Yes*. As worship let out we fed the dogs and high-tailed it back to Austin, letting Cristy know we'd arrive around 9:00.

Dad was the same as that afternoon, rattle and all. He slept and peed once or twice, waking just enough to smile up at us and roll his eyes backward, back to sleep. It was a look as if saying *I'm heading on out and from what I've seen so far it aint like Sunday school but it's wonderful...*

Kim and I had a window of time until about midnight before we'd have to head home and care for the dogs. We visited with Cristy and the night aide, giving Dad his meds every hour or so, fueling his tank for his travels.

Midnight came and I gave Kim the nod that we needed to head south. Another coffee for the road and we were in the truck. Merle didn't make that late-night trip. As we buckled up I leaned over to Kim and said "Wouldn't it be cool if Dad passed at

4:32?"

"It would be creepy...but really cool" looking at me like *I hope that happens...*

4:32

B ack in 1993 some weird things happened, things that would get weirder as time went on. Dad got lonely quickly, remarried seventeen short months after Mom passed and lived somewhere in the northeast for a year or two, before relocating to San Antone, as he called it. He had officially retired from CE, after an acquisition, and began consulting while redesigning a second attempt at full-retirement. Having him close-by, we were around him more often, and that was a good thing, most of the time.

I had been reassigned to a business development position and travelling non-stop, as we do in that line of work.

Dad's wife had given me a Christmas gift, a cheap, plastic, imitation watch of some sort that I wore strictly out of respect for Dad; *just keeping it real.*

Developing a project in northern Arizona required frequent travel there and many late nights at the office as we prepared to bid the job. For no reason that I know of, I began waking up, alarm clock-less, at the same time every morning, 4:32 AM. This went on for a couple of days with no thought about it, but when it continued for the next few weeks, it got my attention.

What's up with 4:32 AM? I began to wonder. *I could use another hour in the racks.* After a few weeks of this, *What's up?* became *What the...?*

During those weeks, one night I dreamed deeply; more of a vision I'd later realize. Clear as day I dreamed that my brother, sister and I stood a hundred yards back from a shoreline, on a sandy beach I'd never seen. Cloudless and bright as it could be was that day, the weather mild and comfortable, breezeless, unlike any beach I'd been to.

An old-fashioned, wooden lifeguard stand stood at the shoreline, painted in pastel stripes. Expecting Frankie Avalon and Annette Funicello to Beach Blanket Bingo their way across the screen, I dreamed on. A weathered beach house, filled with a gathering of people, that crowd that shows up in your dreams that you've never met but feel that you should know. Yep, they were all in there but we couldn't have cared less about them; we were fixated on the distant shoreline.

A slim figure stood at the shoreline, in white t-shirt, khaki shorts, his bare feet just at the water's edge, ankle-deep...longingly looking at three figures in the water, floating in black, rubber inner tubes (old school). Even from the distance, I recognized them all; Dad at the shoreline, a married couple, Jack and Rheba Mims, close friends of our parents'...and Mom.

I'd seen these two couples together hundreds of times in real life, as our family lake cabins were close together. The four of them had floated like this many a summer afternoon on Lake Travis. But this time, like a kid left out at recess, watching the others play, Dad stood on the shoreline, longing to be with them, once again, but couldn't. Ever so close, but too far away. Those three had gone on before him and he longed to be where they were...he missed her more than we would ever know.

I've seen Caddy Shack 182 times but can recall this vision in greater detail than that movie. I cherished it then and even more today. I woke from this dream at 4:32 AM, knowing without a shadow of doubt where Dad's heart was and where he wanted to be again, next to her.

That morning I dressed and drove to the airport for my flight to Phoenix, hustling to navigate the airport parking, long walk to the terminal, security checkpoints, etc. I checked my watch, the cheap, plastic one, to see if I had time for a coffee before takeoff...It had stopped...at 4:32 that morning. If I'm lying I'm dying.

What the...? then went straight to *Holy shit!*

Telling my coworker, travel partner and friend, Steve, what had happened he didn't want to travel with me. I didn't want to travel with me either! We then checked our plane ticket to confirm we weren't on flight 432. We would've cancelled the trip without thinking twice.

26 years later I haven't awakened again at 4:32; I check every time. I've wondered for years what it could have meant...

Kim and I made it home from Austin and hit the hay around 2:30 that Sunday morning, July 22nd. We slept for about an hour before my mobile rang...

"Hey Johnboy..." said Cristy. "...The nurse says she can't find a pulse...We think Dad might be gone..." her voice cracking. "...She's calling the head nurse..."

Kim was up and half-dressed as I said "We're on our way"

Leaving the neighborhood, I called the head hospice nurse, who was also in route to Dad's. "Hey there...We got the call...Yep... You heading there now?...OK...Us too...We will...You too...Are you the one who will pronounce him?...OK...That's what I thought...Go ahead and do what you need to do but can you hold off on calling Weed-Corley until we get there?...We'd like to spend some time with him before he goes with them...Thanks... OK...See you there...Bye"

We drove to Austin like we had driven to Dallas thirty one years before, making record time. Traffic is a non-issue on I-35 that time of the morning. Pulling into the exact parking spot we had left just a few hours before, we arrived at his apartment around

5:15. The hallway from the elevators to his apartment seemed about as long as that cold, sterile one at Parkland Hospital.

Opening the door we were quietly, somberly greeted by Paul, Cristy, the night aide and the head hospice nurse. Entering Dad's room, he was right where we had left him, although a lot more relaxed. Like *an empty shell, dishabited,* his lifeless body lay dead-still with a peaceful countenance like I'd never seen on him. We loved on him, talked to him and kissed his forehead, respectfully and full of gratitude.

Then, I broke the sadness with "The clock starts now...He gave us only two hours to cry and that's it!" We all laughed aloud. Dad even tried to control our grief. *Good luck with that, Dad... We're on our own now...*

Returning to the living, now awaiting Weed-Corley (Thurlow couldn't make it) we sat and made small talk, like you do in times like that. The nurse stood in the entryway, just behind me, watching for the undertakers' down the hallway.

Leaning back I asked "Did you pronounce him?" "Yes sir, I did" she said respectfully, hospice-like. "What time did you pronounce him?" "It was 4:30" she replied curiously. "Are you sure it wasn't 4:32?" I asked, eyebrows raised, smiling in anticipation.

"Oh...No sir...It was 4:30. After checking all vitals and confirming his condition, I looked at my iPhone and it said 4:30" she replied gently, but certainly.

I smiled, looking at Kim, shrugging my shoulders "Ehhh...It was close" to which she smiled back.

The room was looking at me with eager curiosity as if *Is there more to that story?* to which I said "It's nothing...Something I'll tell you about another time". The room fell silent for a few seconds...

"But the clock on his nightstand read 4:32" she added.

I smiled at Kim, as she smiled in return "Of course it did...Of course it did" and we left it at that.

The young woman and man in black arrived, velvet sleeping-bagged gurney in tow and greeted us, mortician-like, before disappearing into Dad's room, closing the door behind them, as they do.

Respectfully escorting them back down the hallway, to the elevator and out past the mail slots, where we'd picked up his mail a thousand times, out the glass door, down the sidewalk ramp for the disabled and to their awaiting, unmarked, white van. The timing was good. Too early for most of the Conservatory residents to be out and about; the perfect time for E.S. Hornsby to slip out unnoticed.

We hugged and thanked the nurse and the aide, making one more coffee for the road and headed to our respective homes, preparing for the days ahead. Cristy stayed there.

The peace that surpasses all understanding drove us home. All was right...right where he needed to be. Did we cry? Of course...for a couple of hours...then we cried as we needed to, not as we were told to.

THURLOW'S PLACE

T hurlow had his place set up just right, just as Dad wanted, like an over-sized living room; early '70s Americana with plenty of space for everyone to spread out and visit; no one held hostage in a long receiving line, stuck between couples you'd rather not talk to, just as Dad requested, minus the wine.

We'd spread pictures here and there, as if it was our own living room, for the guests to enjoy. One, in particular gave us a good laugh, as we displayed it and explained it throughout the evening. It was a brown and white, sepia-looking, photo of Dad and one of his Navy buddies with two girls whom we'd never seen nor heard of. Dad held onto the picture all these years for some reason…so we thought it would be funny to display. The smirk on Dad's face says it all…we'll leave it at that.

We spread out and "worked the crowd" as Dad would say, visiting with Dad's friends, our friends, distant family members and the like who showed up to pay their respects to Dad…and us. It meant a lot to us all. Just as Dad requested, he was over in the corner, his wood, orange and white rose sprayed, longhorn logoed casket appropriately positioned, lid shut tight. The event was all *about* him…yet all *for* us…just as he had designed.

As closing time drew near, Dad's last "Last Call" came, we reboxed the pictures and did a final walkthrough, stopping by his box one last time for the evening. We'd see him once more out at Austin Memorial early the next morning.

Simply rubbing the edge of the smooth wood Johnboy who'd lost his Dad had a tender moment, but I left it there so Reverend John could step-up the next morning...and there was *no way* I was getting those two mixed up at his graveside.

My lifelong friend, Gready, stood by my side that entire evening, as lifelong friends do. Stopping me before we left for the evening, he looked me right in the eye and shared a most profound truth, "John, a boy becomes a man when his Dad dies...Remember that" as he hugged the life out of me, as lifelong friends do.

Reverend John had but one more appearance to make and Johnboy could take it from there. I needed those words from my friend. The graveside would require the man Dad needed me to be...and that Mom had birthed me to be.

Dad's funeral planning was paying off in spades; visitation had gone perfectly and the graveside service was coming together as well. He had warned me about others wanting to "preach a little", and he was right; I "bounced" them like I said I would.

A beautiful morning arose, unseasonably cooler than normal and a good-sized crowd of loved ones gathered round for The Eagle's final landing.

15 minutes meant 15 minutes, so we kept it at that. I spoke a few words about death, burial and resurrection (as we pastors do) as the gravediggers lowered him into the ground. They honored our request to do so.

Paul shared a few good words from Lonesome Dove before Dad's congregational pastor, who'd been invited, and limited, by me, to a 60-second prayer with no hint of evangelical innuendo, closed out the service in perfect alignment with Dad's wishes.

As "the guy next door" moved in, I couldn't help but notice the size of the gathered loved ones there, one of which caught my eye. White dress shirt, jeans, boots, tears streaming from beneath his sunglasses. I couldn't make him out but he held my attention as the closing prayer came to its close.

Also at our request, a mound of dirt was left by the gravediggers, along with a few shovels. I invited anyone and everyone the privilege of burying Dad. Some did, some respectfully observed and others made their way to their vehicles. That kind of thing isn't for everyone. The little ones, great grandchildren of Big Ed's, stood at the grave barrier looking directly into the grave, watching every move. Oh, if we would grieve as honestly and matter-of-factly as little children...

"...unless you change and become like little children, you'll never see the kingdom..."

Jesus

It was quiet...reverent...special.

I made a beeline for the guy in white, introducing myself, assuming we'd never had the privilege. Removing his shades, through his tear-filled eyes, I recognized him right away...It was Danny Quinlan. I couldn't believe it. We hadn't seen each other since the final game after I went 0 for 4. He'd heard about Dad's passing and made the trip. Danny threw the first shovel-full into Dad's grave. He will never know what it meant to me for him to be there; it meant the world to Dad as well. He always, always had a fondness for Danny.

As we scooped the last shovelful into his grave, the crowd began to disperse with hugs and low-hanging heads. I remained behind.

Standing alone, at the grave I'd visited regularly for the past year and a half, looking six-feet down. There they were, together again. The scraped edge of Mom's container exhumed just enough for me to see. It'd been nearly 31 years. I'd longed to see it just once more. Now, standing above them both I thought how good it might feel to drop down in there and lay between them, like I used to…but I no longer felt the need to.

Feeling like a little boy, yet, strangely, more like a man than ever before, I just stood there…looking at them…

Without thinking, in one fluid motion, instinctively I drew deep into the front pocket of my jeans and pulled a coin, the coin I'd been carrying there for the past few months, and flipped it, high, heads-tails-heads-tails-heads-tails…into his grave, watching it instantly disappear under the powdered soil…Gone.

I thanked them both and, walking away, I whispered *It is finished. Gready was right.*

Together again
My tears have stopped falling
The long lonely nights
Are now at an end

Together again
The gray skies are gone
You're back in my arms
Now where you belong

The love…
The love that I knew
Is living again

And nothing else matters
We're together again

Buck Owens

EPILOGUE

I'm a couple of months shy of 56 years old and just now figured out who I am. As you've now read, it took a lot of years, some deep soul searching, a damn-good spiritual guru and the voice of my not-as-dead-as-I-thought Mom to get me there. I pray you find yourself a lot sooner.

The *narrow way that few ever find* is the path that got me there. That narrow way, the pressing way as it's better translated, is on the underside of those smelly pew cushions I talked about. See for yourself.

Like a fat dude squeezing down a small pipe, the leaner I get the further down the *way* I go. *Strip off the weight that holds you back* the Good Book says. Large loads aint for narrow roads (I just made that up).

And, I'm finding out, the dark glass aint as dark down the *narrow way. Face-to-face and knowing as I'm fully known* is clearing things up pretty good, even without morphine. *My walk is truly getting closer and closer to Thee.*

So, who am I?

I'm not in as big a hurry as I once was and life's a lot simpler than I once knew. I'm a creative, imaginative, spontaneous dreamer who sees life like he sees it. I love strippers and California drifters, tattoos and their artists, am transparent to a fault and demand the same from you in return.

I'm immature, fearless, restless and a bit reckless. I'm a student of the Spirit and hear its voice from the bodhisattvas, medicine men, holy men and psychopomp soul guides that help me along the way. Look it up.

I love my wife as Christ loved the church, love my ever-growing family and love *Love* when I see it in its pure form, no matter *who* it is loving *who*.

I've *never* liked the taste of venison but ate it until Mom died. I don't kill *anything* just for the sake of killing it. A good cigar sometimes grabs me and I still love the *passive* smell of weed. I'm still an alcoholic and still stay sober one day at a time. I have more tattoos than ever, with more on the way. I cuss a little, speak truth with love more often and still convince myself people can't see me picking my nose while I drive.

I love *all* people, but have less and less time for closeminded bullshit and religious nonsense; Hell, I have no stone to throw; I used to be one. I wear pointy-toed boots and Birdwells (not together) and I have more hair in my ears than my head and I fart involuntarily more often...and don't care.

I love Dad, for he was, is and all he did for us. He loved us wholeheartedly. Dad, I learned more from you than you'll ever know...well you probably *do* know now.

I love Jesus more than ever and I love life... but I love death even more and put myself to death a little more each day...and I look forward to *life over yonder*...when my time comes.

I love Mom and the *narrow way* she showed me and that's led me to who *I am*...and where I've learned with blessed assurance that the tattoo artist wasn't talkin' about my Ichthys sticker...

That's who I am...Who are you?

Love you, Mom and Dad.

Until face-to-face,

John M. Hornsby

John ("Reverend John" to you, Dad)

A WORD FROM CLO

My sweet son, there hasn't a day gone by that I haven't been right beside you all. I know you can't see me and it feels like I'm a million miles away...but I'm right here with you, always have been, always will be...Lo, I will be with you alway, even unto the end of the world...and, at that time, we will be together again, forever. I can't wait!

That day in Dallas was sad for me too. That little blood vessel just didn't cooperate; now did it? Jesus caught me and held that evening, as he always has in one way or another, and he holds you all too. My heart was broken for you all that day in Dallas and the years after.

I was there with you as Kim held your arm in my hospital room; she is a dear and the answer to our prayers for you. My loving arms were around your broken hearts that day, yours, Kim's, Cristy's and Paul's, trying my best to hold y'all together.

Your Father always leaned on me, as I always leaned on him. With me gone, he was lost, like he was when he and I first met. He's never felt safe alone. I tried to comfort him but hearing and seeing me in our house was too much for him and he had to leave. I understood, but I know it was hard on you all, especially his last 29 years.

Your father and I love you all so very much...and have since we first laid eyes on you. He and I came together in God's perfect timing and tried our best to build a life together and a home for you all. We were just kids, trying to create something neither of us ever had. We love our families and are thankful for them (see them every day now) but wanted to do what we felt God wanted for us; we gave it our best, though imperfectly much of the time. I hope you all can find it in your hearts to forgive our shortcomings.

I have a much-better understanding of the Bible now, as you can imagine; it's much clearer up here. Ha. Proverbs 22:6 has been written to say "Train up a child in the way he should go and when he is old, he will not depart from it". Your Father interpreted this his way and I did my way. He understood that he should "Show you the way", and I understood it, and still do, as "Help a child find their way". I watched him show you his way and I watched you, painfully, try to live into that. I called you back to me now to give you a fresh start, to born you again. I know the little precious boy I gave birth to and want you to discover that...You're well on your way and I'm so excited for you!

You were so young but do you remember when I told you about that musical group that was in the airplane accident? They had so much more to say...and so did I. Like many of us here, we were too young... They were over for supper the other evening! When I told them about our reconnection they wanted me to remind you...

> *Come sit beside me my son and listen closely to what I say*

> *Oh, take your time, don't live too fast. Troubles will come and they will pass*

> *You'll find a woman and you'll find love, and don't forget, son, there is someone up above"*

> *Forget your lust for the rich man's gold - All that you need is in your soul*

Such sweet young men they are...I just love them!

Cristy, Paul, you and Kim were wonderful for your Father, as he was preparing to come here. You should hear him talk about you! Wasn't he so funny through all of that? He hadn't changed a bit, being in such a hurry to get somewhere. Ha.

As your Mother and someone who's gone on before you, know this;

God is real, Gods love you just like you are and God will never leave you, nor forsake you. God is with you even when it feels like he isn't...and when you wished he wasn't. God does have a place prepared for you and it's wonderful – You should see mine! The drapes are fabulous! Your Father was right; it's not like Sunday School and my Daddy taught us...It's even better! Ha.

Well, I'd better get back to the group...It's swim day and my inner tube awaits me.

Love always and forever...See you before you know it,

Mom

THE LETTERS

As the final touches were put on this memoir, while reading the last of those college letters between Mom and Dad, I rose from the bed, foggy-eyed and half-asleep and yelled "Are you kidding me!!!!!!" at the top of my lungs.

Eddie, a.k.a "Smoky" had written to his "Sweet Clo" "Sug" and "Best gal" late one evening telling her he was failing...let me get this right...Chemistry, English and Physics one semester at Texas University (as they called it back then) and took some time off from school going back after they were married.

Oscar Wilde had it right;

Every Saint has a past and every sinner has a future

E.S. Hornsby was saint-like in the image he portrayed throughout his adult life, but apparently that "saint" had a past and it felt good to know that; would've felt even better about 50 years ago. Would've loosened the boards of The Box.

As lay back in the bed, I laughed to myself, and nodded *I finally get...It all makes sense.*

My once weary soul rested well that night knowing my "saint" had a past...and *I* have a future. Hearing someone failed never felt so good...

You were right, Cristy...I'm *thanking you later*.

p.s.

"Sug, you kept all those letters?" "Yes, Smoky, I gave them to Cristy because I knew she would keep them and you'd just throw them away" "But..." "Buts have no place up here...Let it go, Smoky...Let it go..."

On my run "Home"

Jerry a.k.a. The Master

Merle's Heart of Gold

Day One

Enough Said...

56483157R00093

Made in the USA
Columbia, SC
25 April 2019